Keep Your Marine Diesel Running

Richard Thiel

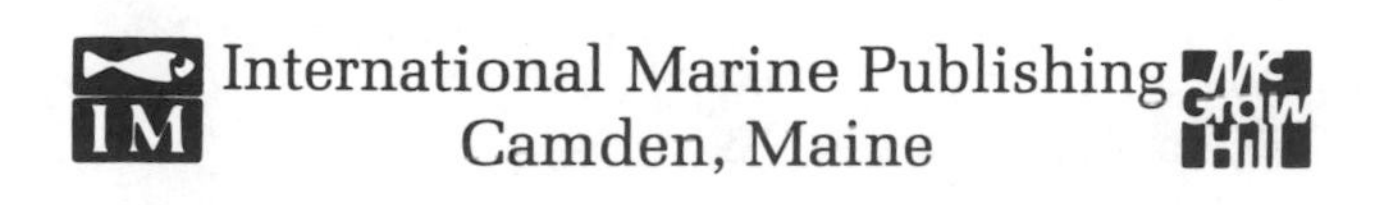

Acknowledgments

Many thanks to everyone who provided art for this book — especially Skip Arnold at Caterpillar, Inc.; Peter Cote at Jordan-Milton Machinery; and all the folks at Detroit Diesel.

Published by International Marine
10 9 8 7 6 5 4 3 2 1

TAB BOOKS is a division of McGraw-Hill, Inc.

Library of Congress Cataloging-in-Publication Data.
Thiel, Richard, 1945–
Keep your marine diesel running / by Richard Thiel.
p. cm.
Includes index.
ISBN 0-87742-266-4
1. Marine diesel motors—Maintenance and repair. I. Title.
VM770.T44 1991
621.43'58—dc20 90-22748
CIP

TAB BOOKS offers software for sale. For information and a catalog, please contact TAB Software Department, Blue Ridge Summit, PA 17294-0850.

Questions regarding the content of this book should be addressed to:

International Marine Publishing
P.O. Box 220
Camden, ME 04843

Imageset by High Resolution, Camden, ME
Printed by Arcata Graphics, Fairfield, PA
Design by Faith Hague, Watermark Design, Camden, ME
Pagination by Faith Hague, Watermark Design, Camden, ME
Edited by J.R. Babb, Heidi N. Brugger
Production by Janet Robbins

CONTENTS

Introduction

The purpose of this book is to give you brief and painless explanations of how your marine diesel works, how to operate it, and how to take care of it. Once you know the basics, you'll be able to reason through your own maintenance and operational program, and deal intelligently with a technician when you need one.

This book is written for someone who knows absolutely nothing about engines of any kind, and equally important, someone who has little or no interest in them other than making sure they serve him well. In short, it is a basic survival manual for the diesel boat operator.

This book is *not* about how to conduct major repairs or how to rebuild a diesel in your bedroom using just a hammer and a screwdriver. In fact, you'll find few, if any, references to actually fixing a diesel here. Instead, the emphasis will be on preventing problems from occurring in the first place.

Why? Because in spite of what you may have read or been told to the contrary, the diesel engine is an enormously complex piece of machinery, much more so than a gasoline engine under a car's hood. Unless you are a man or woman of unusual mechanical aptitude and you have a large assortment of specialized tools, you'll be far better off leaving significant repairs to someone who has undergone extensive training in the art (yes, it is an art) of repairing a diesel engine. (Frustrated shade-tree mechanics who can't leave well-enough alone or who plan on frequenting areas devoid of diesel mechanics should read *Marine Diesel Engines—Maintenance, Troubleshooting and Repair*, by Nigel Calder, International Marine Publishing, 1987).

Besides, the marine diesel is a very reliable engine—again, more so than an automobile's gasoline engine. If you maintain and operate your diesel properly, you should have years of trouble-free operation before you have to call on a mechanic.

In addition to learning the basics of engine operation, this book will guide you in choosing spare parts and tools that should be aboard at all times. Few of either are really necessary, but having the right ones aboard could save you a lot of grief someday.

And finally, this book will provide a basic lesson in the art of troubleshooting, a skill you'll need not only to fix the small problems, but to enable you to deal intelligently with the person you hire to fix the big ones. By applying the principles of troubleshooting and the basic working knowledge of the diesel you will have gleaned from the first chapters, you will—believe it or not—be able to reason through most maladies before having to call an expert.

A marine engine represents a significant portion of the total cost of any boat; a marine diesel engine, even more so. A good diesel technician—if you can find one—typically will charge at least $40 an hour, and it takes a lot of time to work on a marine diesel. Moreover, diesel parts typically are at least half-again as expensive as similar parts for a gasoline engine.

Frightening? It should be, but consider this. If properly maintained, the average marine diesel engine should and will far outlast the hull in which it is installed. Unlike its gasoline counterparts, the marine diesel is almost always based upon a commercial engine, perhaps one designed to power a truck, bus, or generator. It probably was designed from the ground up to last not hundreds but thousands of hours, without a lot of attention. Likewise, if you take care of the diesel in your boat, it will last virtually indefinitely. You'll end up either willing it to your heirs or, more likely, selling the boat long before you need to rebuild or replace the engine.

Giving you a working knowledge that allows you to maximize the trouble-free life of your diesel engine is what this book is all about.

PART ONE

How the Marine Diesel Works

The Internal Combustion Engine

The diesel engine in a boat and the gasoline engine in a car have a lot in common. Each is termed an **internal combustion engine** because it burns fuel inside itself to produce power, as opposed to an **external combustion engine**, such as the steam engine, which burns fuel outside itself. The following description applies *both* to the car's gasoline engine and the boat's diesel engine.

The Basic Parts

The basic component of an internal combustion engine is the **engine block**, basically a chunk of cast iron into which **cylinders** have been drilled. The cylinders may be configured in a single row, in which case the engine is called an **in-line**, or they may be arranged in two rows separated by anywhere from 60° to 90°, in which case the engine is called a **V**. Thus, if both kinds of engines had six cylinders, one would be called an in-line six and the other would be called a V-6.

Inside each cylinder is a **piston**, basically a slug of metal slightly smaller than the cylinder so that it can slide up and down. It contains two or three grooves in its circumference into which are fit resilient, metal **piston rings** that press up against the walls of the cylinders, creating a seal.

Each block has a top, fashioned so that each cylinder has a sealed space on top of its piston. This top, called the **cylinder head**, is secured by bolts and sealed to the block with a **gasket**. The area left between each piston and the cylinder head is called the **combustion chamber**. Although the piston moves up and down the cylinder, it never travels all the way to the top and touches the cylinder head;

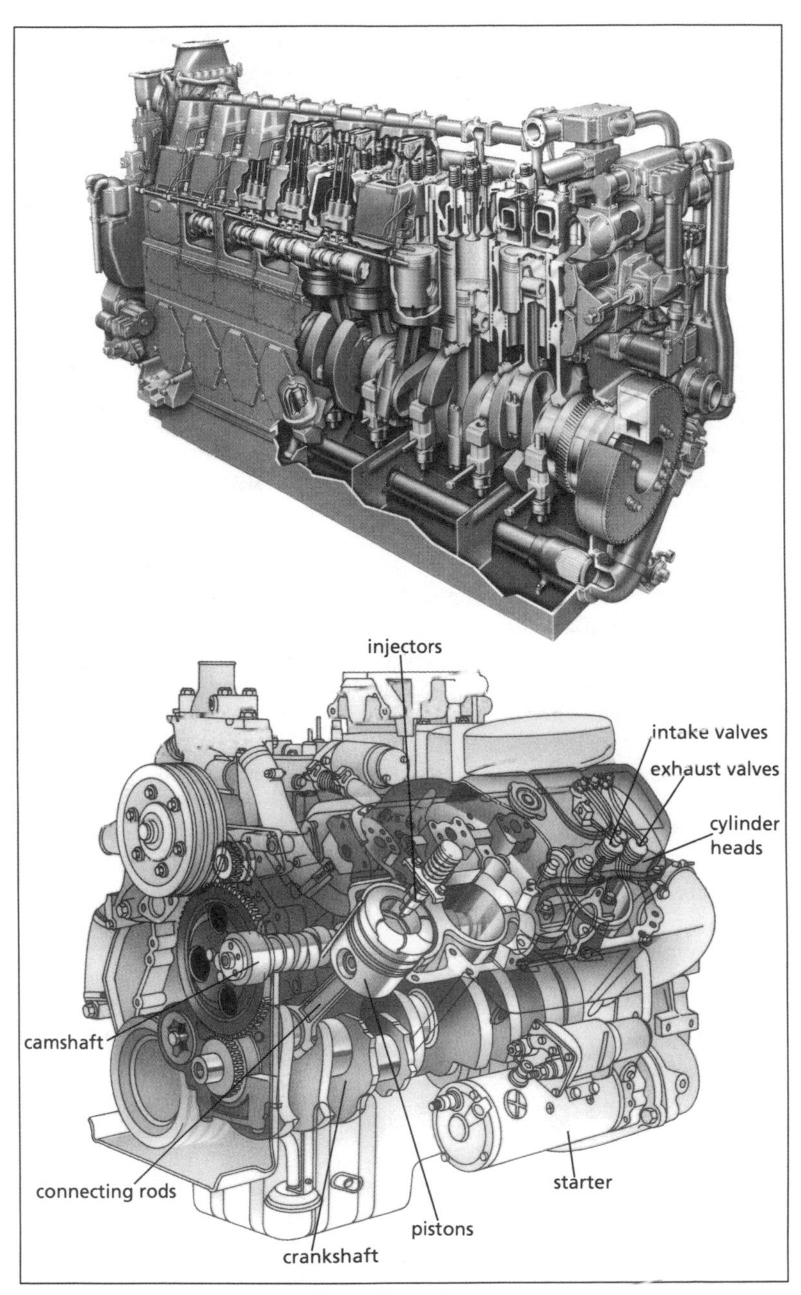

Figure 1-1 In-line (top) and V (bottom) diesels.

there is always a small area left between piston and cylinder head, and that is where fuel is burned to produce power.

Compression in a Gasoline Engine

If you were to measure the area of the combustion chamber when the piston is at the bottom of its travel and compare it with the area left when the piston is at the top of its travel, you would come up with a pair of numbers called the **compression ratio**. For instance, in an engine with a nine-to-one (written as 9:1) compression ratio, each piston leaves nine times more space when it's at the bottom of the cylinder than when it's at the top. As we'll see, the size of the compression ratio is one of the critical differences between a gasoline and a diesel engine.

Regardless of whether we're speaking of a fireplace or a boat engine, the object is the same: to produce heat through the burning or combustion of fuel. All combustion requires three things: fuel, oxygen, and heat. In your fireplace, that usually means room air, wood, and a match.

To make combustion occur in an internal combustion engine we need to admit fuel, either gasoline or diesel, and fresh air into the combustion chamber. Once both are there in the proper proportions, we then must supply a heat source to ignite the two. How we supply the heat source is another critical difference between the gasoline engine and the diesel engine. In a gasoline engine, the heat source is provided by an electrical spark jumping across the poles of a spark plug.

If you were to place a small amount of gasoline in a bowl in the presence of fresh, oxygenated air and touch a match to it, you'd get rapid combustion. Although the gasoline on top would burn first and that on the bottom might only burn partially or not at all because air can't reach it, heat still would be produced that theoretically could be used to perform some kind of work.

But if you took the same amount of gasoline and sprayed it into the air so that each droplet were surrounded by fresh air—in other words, if you *atomized* the gasoline—you'd get much more uniform and complete combustion, and therefore produce significantly more heat per unit of fuel.

Now imagine spraying an atomized mixture of gasoline and air inside a cylinder when the piston is roughly at the bottom of its travel, then sealing the space, and squeezing the mixture to, say, one-ninth its original volume. When you ignited it with a spark plug this time, you'd have produced a good deal more heat out of the same amount of fuel.

But you'd have to be careful, because when you compress air, you raise its temperature. If you squeeze a mixture of gasoline and air too much, it will ignite at the wrong time from the heat produced by compression, not from the heat of a spark plug. If combustion occurs too soon, while the piston is still on its way up, you get *detonation*, which in extreme cases can blow a hole right through the piston.

Oil companies put additives in gasoline to make it resist such spontaneous ignition, a characteristic that is reflected in gasoline's **octane** rating. But even with high-octane gasoline, 10:1 is about the highest compression ratio possible today without causing damage.

Compression in a Diesel Engine

A basic difference between a diesel engine and a gasoline engine is that a diesel doesn't compress a mixture of air and fuel, just air. Without fuel, combustion cannot occur, so a diesel can compress air to say, one-twentieth its volume and produce only heat—a lot of heat. The temperature of the air inside the cylinder of a typical diesel with a 20:1 compression ratio is approximately 1,500°F. This compressed air, not an electrical spark, is the diesel's heat source.

Only after the air is fully compressed and heated to such a level is diesel fuel sprayed into the combustion chamber. When the fuel comes into contact with the superheated air, it ignites rapidly and burns almost completely, which explains in part why more heat (and therefore more work) is produced from diesel fuel than from an equivalent measure of gasoline.

There are two types of diesel fuel injection: direct and indirect. Direct injection sprays fuel into the combustion chamber, the area between the piston at the top of its travel and the cylinder head. Indirect injection, in contrast, uses a small pre-chamber that is machined into the cylinder head and connected to the combustion chamber by a passage. Fuel is first injected into the pre-chamber, and it is here that combustion begins. As the fuel burns, it expands and rushes out into the main chamber, forcing down the piston. Most pre-chamber diesels have a small heating element or glow plug to help start the engine when it is cold. Thus, most pre-chamber diesels have a light on their instrument panel to indicate that the glow plug is hot enough for the engine to start. Because the pre-chamber adds more surface area to the cylinder, pre-chamber diesels are easier to start than direct injection diesels. But that greater surface area also provides more chance for the exhaust gases to cool as they expand; pre-chamber diesels are not as fuel efficient as direct injection engines, and they are being phased out.

High compression ratios may make for better fuel efficiency, but they also generate greater forces that can tear an engine apart. This is why a diesel runs more roughly and is noisier than a gasoline engine, and why it must be stronger and heavier.

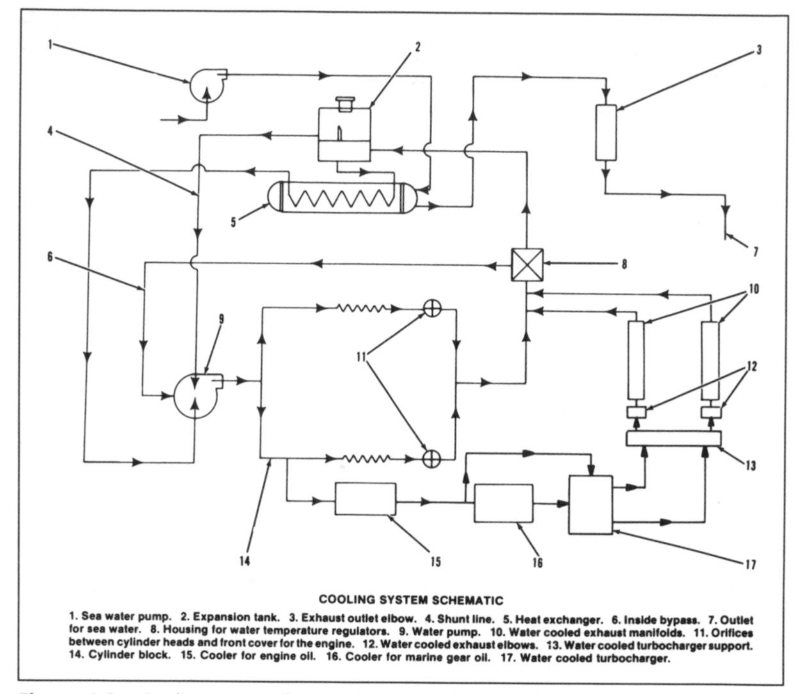

Figure 1-2 Cooling system for a turbocharged marine diesel.

The Rest of the Story

Regardless of whether it's from gasoline or diesel, the heat produced in an engine's combustion chamber generates expansion, forcing the piston down the cylinder. Each piston is connected to a **connecting rod**, which has a hole on each end. One end pivots on a horizontal shaft going through the piston; the other is connected to a **crankshaft**, which translates the vertical motion of the piston into rotary motion that can be used to turn a wheel, generator, pump, or propeller.

To make any engine last, two things must be controlled: friction and heat. Too much of either will quickly destroy an engine. To control heat, blocks and cylinder heads are constructed with internal voids through which liquid is circulated by a belt-driven pump. The coolant is routed eventually to a radiator or some other form of heat exchanger to dissipate heat. This is the **cooling system**.

You may think that the more heat that can be removed from an engine the better, but that isn't so. Remember that the purpose of the entire internal combustion process is to generate heat that can be put to work. If an engine runs too cold, the walls of its combustion chamber

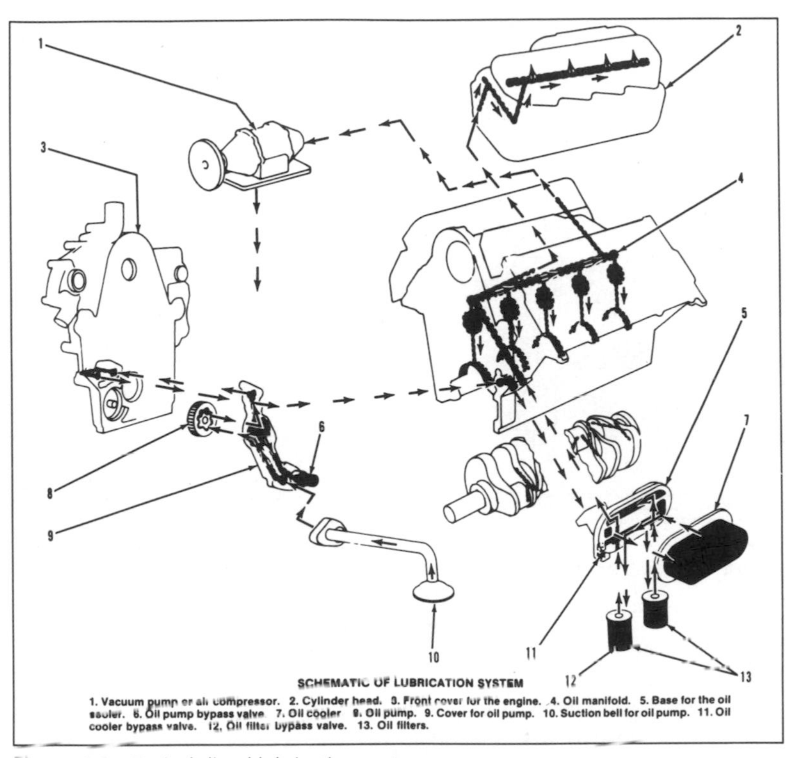

Figure 1-3 Typical diesel lubrication system.

will cool or "quench" the expanding gasses and rob the engine of power.

While this can be important in a gasoline engine, it is absolutely crucial in a diesel, which, lacking a spark plug, must depend solely upon the heat generated by compression to ignite the fuel. If its combustion chamber is too cold, the loss of combustion efficiency is much greater. It is obvious what destruction excessive heat can inflict upon a diesel, but a lack of heat can be equally troublesome.

The final component in an internal combustion engine is the **lubrication system**. Both gasoline engines (except for outboards) and diesels rely upon a pool of lubricating oil located in the bottom of the engine or the **crankcase**. This oil, which is either pumped or splashed to all the critical engine components, usually is circulated through a filter to keep it clean.

Diesel lubrication systems differ from those on gasoline engines in two critical ways: First, a diesel generates more heat, so the oil not only must lubricate, but also remove excessive heat from many com-

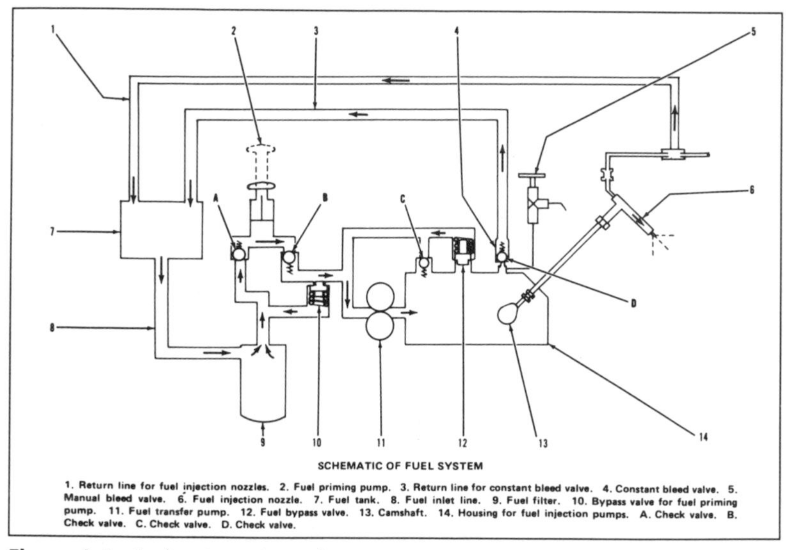

SCHEMATIC OF FUEL SYSTEM

1. Return line for fuel injection nozzles. 2. Fuel priming pump. 3. Return line for constant bleed valve. 4. Constant bleed valve. 5. Manual bleed valve. 6. Fuel injection nozzle. 7. Fuel tank. 8. Fuel inlet line. 9. Fuel filter. 10. Bypass valve for fuel priming pump. 11. Fuel transfer pump. 12. Fuel bypass valve. 13. Camshaft. 14. Housing for fuel injection pumps. A. Check valve. B. Check valve. C. Check valve. D. Check valve.

Figure 1-4 Fuel system schematic.

ponents. For this reason, most diesels are equipped with **oil coolers**, basically heat exchangers that use coolant to remove excessive heat from the oil.

The effectiveness of oil is directly dependent upon its thickness and ability to flow—its **viscosity**— which is partly dependent upon the oil's temperature. If the oil is too cold, it will be too thick and not squeeze into the engine's tiniest spaces; too hot and it will be too thin and be squeezed out of tight spaces. Either way it allows metal to touch metal. A diesel's oil temperature is like its coolant temperature: It must be regulated to within a relatively small range.

Diesel lubrication differs from gasoline engine lubrication in one other crucial way: In order to inject diesel fuel into a highly pressurized combustion chamber at precisely the right moment, a diesel must have a precise **fuel-injection system** that is built to exceedingly close tolerances, tolerances measured not in inches or millimeters but in microns. Of course, the closer together two pieces of metal must operate, the greater the heat generated by friction and the more crucial proper lubrication is.

To keep the fuel-injection system intact, diesel fuel is used not only as a combustible, but as a lubricant. It is circulated around all the critical fuel system components, where its lubricative qualities (which gasoline does not have; gasoline actually is a solvent) help reduce friction. Such qualities are the reason that diesel fuel is heavier and oiler to the touch than gasoline.

More diesel fuel is supplied to the fuel system than it actually needs, and the excess is returned to the fuel tank, carrying with it excessive heat. While gasoline engines have just one line from fuel tank to engine, diesels have two: a **supply line** and a **return line**.

These are the basic components and operating principles of the diesel. Next, we'll look at how the two principal types of diesels operate. They are differentiated by the number of times a piston must travel up and down a cylinder to produce one power stroke. In one type, each piston travels up once and down once to produce a power stroke, and so it is said to use the two-stroke cycle. The engine often is referred to simply as a **two-stroke** diesel.

The other type of diesel requires that each piston travel up twice and down twice to produce one power stroke. It is said to use the four-stroke cycle and often is simply called a **four-stroke** diesel.

For our purposes and to keep things simple, we will say that all two-stroke marine diesels found in noncommercial applications are manufactured by Detroit Diesel. (The company also makes two four-cycle marine diesel V-8s with cylinder displacements of either 6.2 or 8.2 liters.) Virtually all of the marine diesels built by other major manufacturers, such as Caterpillar, Cummins, Volvo Penta, and Perkins, are four-strokes. There are exceptions, but they are not significant within the realm of pleasure boats.

How the Four-Stroke Diesel Works

As the name implies, the four-stroke cycle diesel requires that each piston make four strokes—two up and two down—to generate one stroke of power. While there are wide variations among four-stroke diesels, especially in fuel system design, all follow the basic operating principles outlined below.

Virtually all four-stroke diesels have either two or four **valves** in the cylinder head which, by opening and closing, admit air into and let exhaust gases out of the combustion chamber. Each valve is activated by an eccentric (an egg-shaped lobe) on a **camshaft**, which is gear-driven off the crankshaft. The high spot on the camshaft raises a **push rod** and activates a lever, or **rocker arm**, which depresses and opens the valve. This system ensures that each valve opens and closes at precisely the same point during a piston's trip up and down the cylinder.

The cycle begins with the piston at the top and headed down the cylinder, and with both valves closed. Since it fits tightly within the cylinder, the piston creates a partial vacuum inside the combustion chamber as it moves downward. When the **intake valve** opens early in the piston's journey (the exhaust valve remains closed), outside air rushes in and continues to do so until the piston is roughly at the bottom of its travel. When it reaches this point, the first stroke, or **intake stroke**, is completed.

Somewhere near the bottom of the piston's travel the intake valve closes, sealing the chamber. As the piston moves up the cylinder, it compresses the air, raising its temperature progressively until the piston is roughly at the top of its travel. Thus is completed the second, or **compression, stroke.**

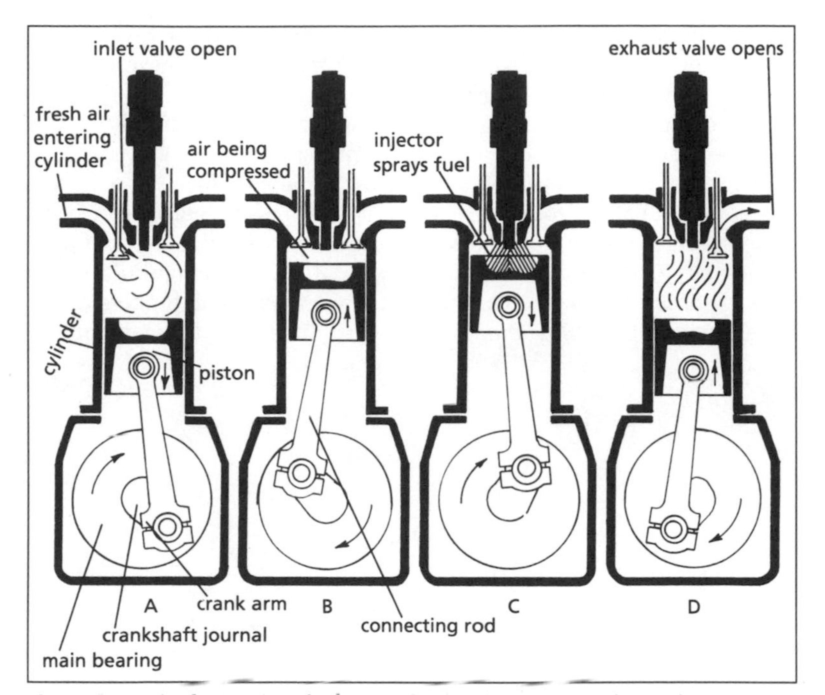

Figure 2-1 The four cycles of a four-stroke diesel engine. A. Inlet stroke. Air is drawn into the cylinder as piston descends. B. Compression. Piston rises, compressing and heating the air. C. Injection. Fuel is sprayed into the hot air, ignites, and burns. The high pressure forces down the piston. D. Exhaust. The spent gases are forced from the cylinder.

When the piston is at the top of its travel (actually, slightly before), a nozzle located in the cylinder head sprays a precisely measured amount of atomized diesel fuel into the combustion chamber. Almost immediately upon contacting the superheated air the fuel burns rapidly and completely, producing heat and causing the gases inside the combustion chamber to expand. The expanding gases force the piston down the cylinder, turning the crankshaft and, eventually, the propeller. Once the piston is near the bottom of the cylinder and the hot gases have cooled and expanded about as far as they can, this expansion stroke, or **power stroke**, is completed. But the cycle isn't over yet.

With the piston now roughly at the bottom of the cylinder, the combustion chamber is full of burned gases that are almost totally lacking in oxygen. Before another power stroke can take place, these gases must be evacuated from the cylinder. To do that, the **exhaust valve** is opened and the piston moves up the cylinder, forcing most of the gases out the open exhaust valve and into the atmosphere. Once the piston is approximately at the top of its travel, this fourth stroke or **exhaust stroke**, is complete, and the cylinder is ready for another charge of fresh air and a new power stroke.

As you can see, in generating a power stroke the engine acts as a pump—an air pump. This is a critical distinction: As we will see, it is fresh air, not fuel, that really determines the power output of a diesel. The advantage of the four-cycle diesel is that it takes two strokes each cycle to actually pump the exhaust gases out of the cylinders and pull in new air. This produces a virtually complete exchange of air and gives the four-cycle diesel superior fuel efficiency. The process of replacing exhaust gas with fresh, oxygenated air is called **scavenging**.

How the Two-Stroke Diesel Works

There are many kinds of two-cycle diesels, each with its own unique design characteristics. Since as pleasure boaters we're unlikely to encounter any but those made by Detroit Diesel, we'll limit our explanation to two-cycles manufactured by that company.

As the name implies, the two-cycle diesel requires only two piston strokes to produce one power stroke. Accomplishing this feat requires that the four events we explained in the previous chapter be combined into two. In fact, in a two-cycle diesel, each upward stroke of a piston is a compression stroke and each downward stroke is a power stroke. Intake and exhaust both occur when the piston is at the bottom of the cylinder. Here's how it works.

We enter the process immediately after combustion has occurred, as the piston is being forced down the cylinder. At this point the combustion chamber is sealed because the four valves—all of which are exhaust valves—are closed. As the piston moves down the cylinder, it uncovers a series of holes, or **ports**, arrayed radially around the walls of the cylinder. The ports of all cylinders lead to a common chamber which is slightly pressurized by a **blower** that is, in turn, mechanically driven by the crankshaft. The blower is clearly visible on the right-hand side of most in-line engines and in the valley between cylinder banks on most V-engines.

When the piston uncovers the cylinder ports, fresh air rushes into the cylinder. At about the same time, the four exhaust valves in the cylinder head open and the exhaust gases are displaced and blown out into the atmosphere by the incoming fresh air. This is the **power stroke**, and at its completion the piston is located roughly at the bottom of the cylinder.

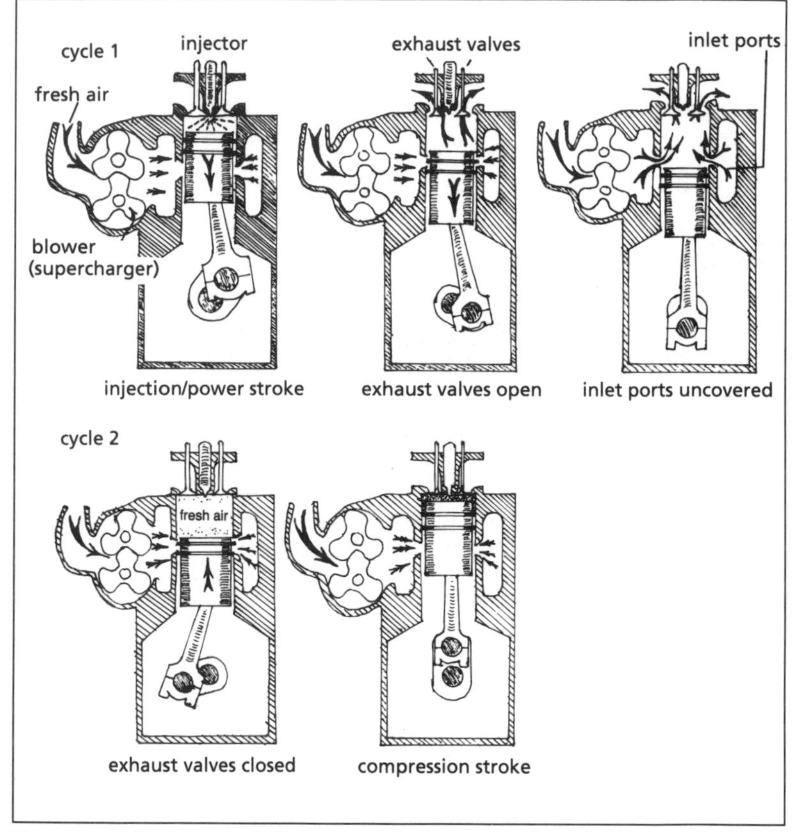

Figure 3-1 The two-stroke cycle of a Detroit Diesel engine.

As the piston begins its upward travel, it passes the intake ports and closes them off. A very short time thereafter (long enough to allow a little more exhaust to escape), the exhaust valves close and the chamber is again sealed. The piston continues upward, compressing the air until it becomes superheated. Just before the piston reaches the top of its travel, diesel fuel is injected into the combustion chamber where it ignites immediately and burns rapidly. The heat of combustion produces expansion and forces the piston down the cylinder, turning the crankshaft and propeller. The piston continues down the cylinder until it again uncovers the intake ports, at which time expansion ceases and the exhaust process begins.

As you can see, the two-stroke cycle is a much simpler system of combustion, and it has the distinct advantage of producing a power stroke twice as frequently as the four-stroke cycle. You might suspect, then, that a two-cycle diesel produces twice the horsepower of an identically sized four-stroke diesel, but that isn't the case.

That's because the power output of any diesel is directly dependent on the amount of air—not fuel—it can pump through each cylinder. The design of the two-cycle diesel allows much less time for exhaust and intake events than that of a four-cycle diesel, hence it can pump less air per stroke. But two-cycles typically *do* put out more horsepower per cubic inch of displacement and per pound of weight than do four-cycle diesels. So the question that obviously follows is, "Why don't all diesels use the two-stroke cycle?"

One answer is fuel efficiency. As we've seen, compared to the four-cycle diesel, a two-cycle diesel allots significantly less time to each combustion event. Specifically, less time is available for pumping out all of the exhaust gasses, which means that a two-cycle diesel typically is not dealing with as clean a charge of air in each combustion chamber as is a four-cycle. Or, as the engineers put it, the scavenging efficiency of a two-cycle is lower than that of a four-cycle. As a result, two-cycle fuel efficiency is somewhat lower than a four-cycle's, although the difference between the two, both in terms of horsepower output and fuel efficiency, seems to be decreasing all the time. Two big reasons for this narrowing gap are **turbocharging** and **intercooling**, which we'll discuss in the next chapter.

Turbocharging and Intercooling

As far as most pleasure boaters are concerned, the more horsepower that can be squeezed out of an engine the better, because less space and weight will be required to achieve a given level of performance. But the diesel engine offers only a few avenues for increasing output. One is to increase cylinder displacement, either by increasing the size of the cylinder bore or the length of the stroke, either of which results in more air being pumped on each stroke. When the amount of fuel injected is increased proportionately, more horsepower will result.

Unfortunately, to get any substantial increase in horsepower, one would also need to significantly increase the exterior dimensions and therefore the weight of an engine. In many cases—and certainly in marine applications—the added bulk and weight of a larger engine would offset much of the increase in horsepower, yielding little or no improvement in either performance or range.

The most practical and cost-effective method for improving the specific output of a diesel is to find some way to make the engine pump more air, which will allow the addition of more fuel. One way to do this is to increase peak operating speed, since the faster a piston moves up and down in its cylinder the more air it will pump. But pistons that move faster also wear more quickly than slower moving ones. And even if you're willing to accept higher wear rates as the price for more power, the amount of increase in peak operating speed is limited by the strength of the components. In relatively short order, engine speed will reach a threshold above which components simply will not hold together.

Fortunately, there is another method of making an engine pump more air: simply force more air into it by using an external pump. Such

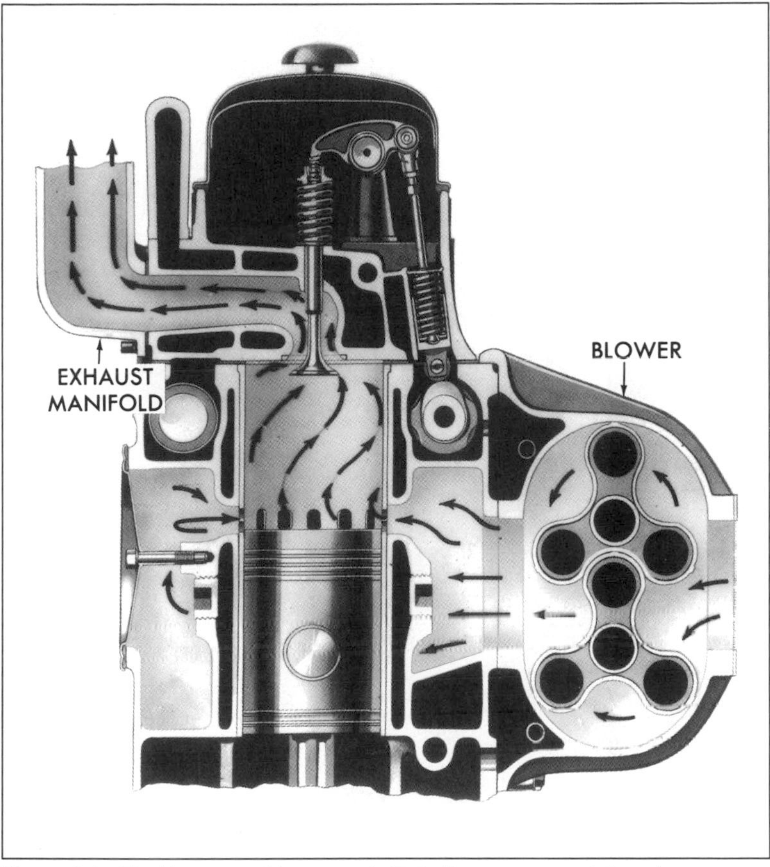

Figure 4-1 The blower on this two-cycle Detroit pumps more air into the combustion chamber than would be drawn in by the descending piston alone.

a pump can have a variety of designs, but generally, if it is connected mechanically to the engine so that it turns at a fixed ratio to the crankshaft, it is called a **supercharger**. Supercharged diesels are virtually unheard-of in marine engines. (The difference between a supercharger and the blower in a two-cycle diesel is one of degree; a blower pumps far less air.) The other method of pumping air into a diesel is by using a **turbocharger**.

Turbocharging

A turbocharger is a relatively simple device composed of two sealed chambers containing complex fan blades, or **turbines**, connected by a shaft. Exhaust passes through the first chamber, which is

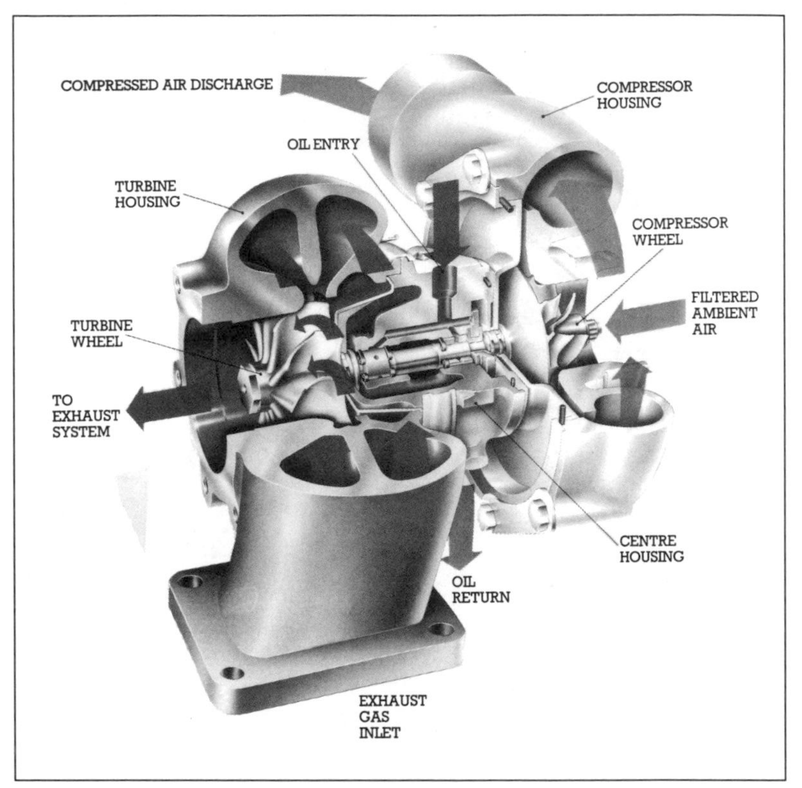

Figure 4-2 Cutaway view of a turbocharger.

made of cast iron and usually is called the **hot side**, shortly after it leaves the cylinders. As you can imagine, the larger the volume of exhaust gasses passing through this chamber, the faster its turbine spins.

The other chamber, made of aluminum and called the **cold side**, draws air in from its center and pumps it through an internal passage of gradually decreasing size, called the **volute**, that ends at the intake manifold. As this turbine, or **compressor**, is spun ever faster by the exhaust turbine, more and more air is forced into the engine. When a sufficient volume of air is pumped into the cylinders so that the pressure there exceeds ambient atmospheric pressure, the turbocharger is said to have generated **boost**, which usually is measured in pounds per square inch.

The area between the hot and cold sides contains a bearing on which runs the shaft that connects the compressor and exhaust turbine. The only thing separating the shaft from the bearing and certain death is a thin film of oil. Both the hot and cold side have seals to prevent oil from leaving the bearing housing or to prevent exhaust or pressurized air from entering it.

The beauty of this system is that waste energy powers the turbocharger, so any horsepower produced is pure gain. Moreover, the flow of exhaust gasses is directly dependent upon the load placed on the diesel. When a diesel is under little or no load, the volume of its exhaust gasses is relatively small and little or no boost is generated. When a load is applied and the throttle is advanced, a higher volume of exhaust gasses is generated. This spins the compressor faster, forcing more air into the cylinders and allowing more fuel to be burned, which produces more horsepower.

The turbocharger is indeed a simple device, but it demands careful manufacture and maintenance for two reasons: First, as you can imagine, it gets very hot; the turbine side typically will reach 800°F under normal operation and more under severe loading. Second, in order to be both responsive and to pump the amount of air necessary, the turbines must spin very fast, sometimes as fast as 100,000 r.p.m., which makes proper lubrication of the connecting shaft crucial.

Even with those drawbacks, the turbocharger has developed into an incredibly reliable, cost-effective piece of equipment, so much so that today the majority of diesel engines in boats are turbocharged. Why? Because the mere application of a turbocharger to a diesel engine can result in an increase in horsepower of as much as 33 percent, with virtually no penalty in reliability and little in longevity. A turbocharged diesel will burn more fuel than one without a turbocharger (called a **naturally aspirated** engine) simply because it is producing more horsepower but, when judged by how much fuel each kind of engine takes to produce one horsepower, the turbocharged engine is actually the more fuel efficient.

Intercooling

Of course, the turbocharged diesel could be better. The single drawback to turbocharging is that any time a gas—in this case air—is compressed, its temperature rises, and the air leaving a typical turbocharger may reach 300°F. That's important for two reasons: First, hot intake air raises temperatures inside the cylinder, an increase that can damage internal components, especially valves and pistons. Second, hot air is less dense that cool air, so while a turbocharger may be pumping mightily, the actual volume of air that goes into the cylinder may amount to a good deal less than it could.

The solution is obvious: Cool the air between the time it leaves the turbocharger and the time it enters the valve passages. Today, that is done by a device that's even simpler than the turbocharger, the **intercooler**, or as it is also known, the **aftercooler**.

There are two methods of intercooling, but both operate in basically the same way: After air exits the turbocharger it passes over a series of tubes and fins containing circulating coolant, located in a device nearly identical to an automotive radiator. The variation derives from the source of the cooling fluid. In most applications, a portion of the engine coolant is diverted to the intercooler, usually right after the coolant leaves the raw-water heat exchanger, which is when it is at its lowest temperature. This low may be around 180°F, thereby providing a substantial temperature reduction in the air, which might otherwise enter at 300°F.

The other system used in high-performance diesels pipes water directly from the engine's raw-water system to the intercooler. Since ambient water is typically between 70° and 80°F, the temperature drop in the intake air is even greater, allowing the use of higher boost pressures without damaging internal components. The disadvantage of raw-water intercooling is that the intercooler may be more subject to corrosion if the boat is operated in polluted or salt water, and that the intercooler's tiny passages may become clogged with suspended material.

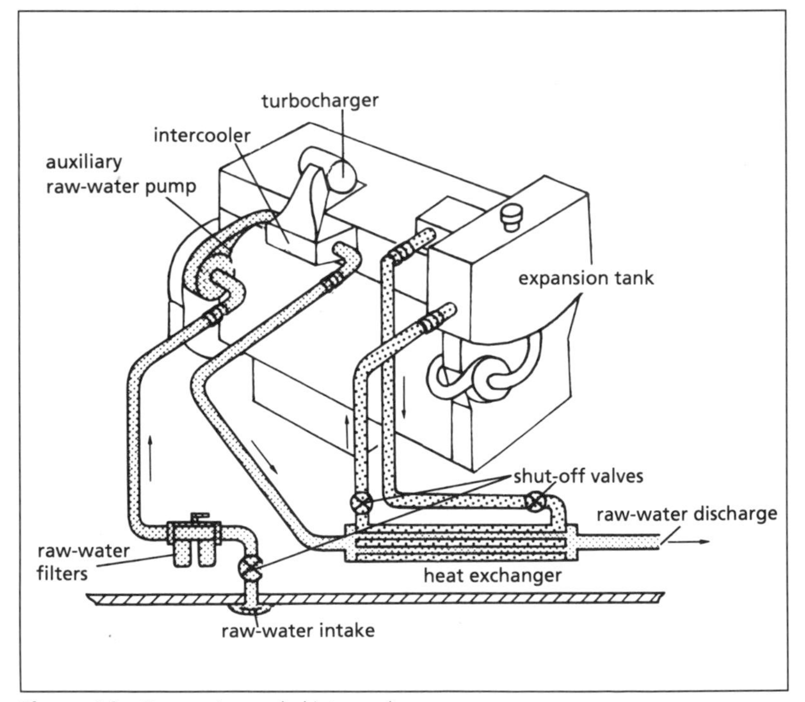

Figure 4-3 Raw-water-cooled intercooler.

The Diesel Fuel System

The primary operating principles of the diesel engine—squeezing air until it is sufficiently hot, then injecting fuel into it—were figured out long ago. The problem from the start was designing a fuel system that could simultaneously accomplish three things: (1) Measure the appropriate amount of fuel to be delivered to each cylinder; (2) Pressurize it

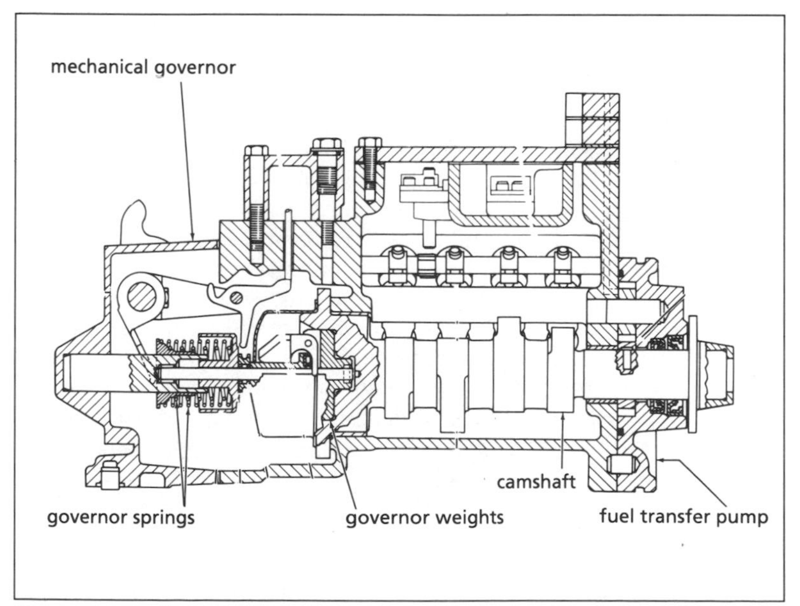

Figure 5-1 Fuel injection pump.

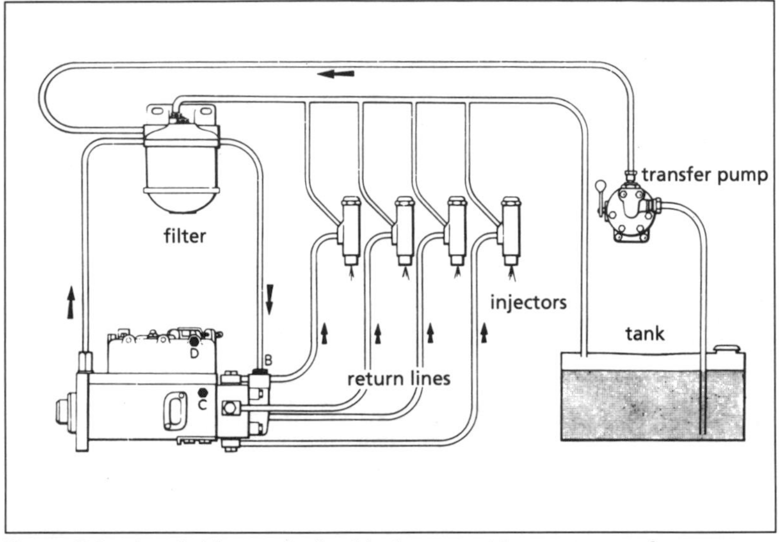

Figure 5-2 A typical four-cycle diesel fuel system with separate transfer pump.

sufficiently to overcome the extremely high pressures present inside the combustion chamber; (3) Atomize the fuel while injecting it into the combustion chamber so that the maximum amount of each fuel charge is burned completely. Once they overcame these early development problems, engineers were able to design and build the modern diesel engine.

For the purposes of this book, there are two basic types of fuel systems in use today aboard pleasure boats: In one, an engine-driven, low-pressure **transfer pump** draws fuel from the tank and supplies it to a larger, centrally located, engine-driven **injection pump** that is responsible for pressurizing and measuring, or **metering**, the fuel. Without getting too involved, this usually is done by a series of small individual plungers (one for each cylinder) located inside the pump, whose range of travel can be varied to modify the amount of fuel dispersed with each stroke. After the fuel is pressurized, it is pumped through steel fuel lines to a nozzle, which typically contains a spring-loaded valve that opens when subjected to sufficient pressure. When the plunger in the injector pump is activated, the valve in the nozzle is unseated, and fuel is atomized and injected into the combustion chamber.

The Unit Injector

The other system, used primarily on Detroit Diesels and some newer Caterpillars, employs a **unit injector**. In this system, an engine-driven, low-pressure transfer pump sends fuel through internal passages, or **galleys**, to one unit injector at each cylinder. Each unit injector is a combination injection pump and nozzle that is mechanically activated by a camshaft-operated valve train. When the camshaft activates the plunger in the top of the unit injector, fuel inside the injector is pressurized and injected into the cylinder. The amount of fuel is determined by the length of the plunger, which is controlled by a mechanical linkage connected to the throttle.

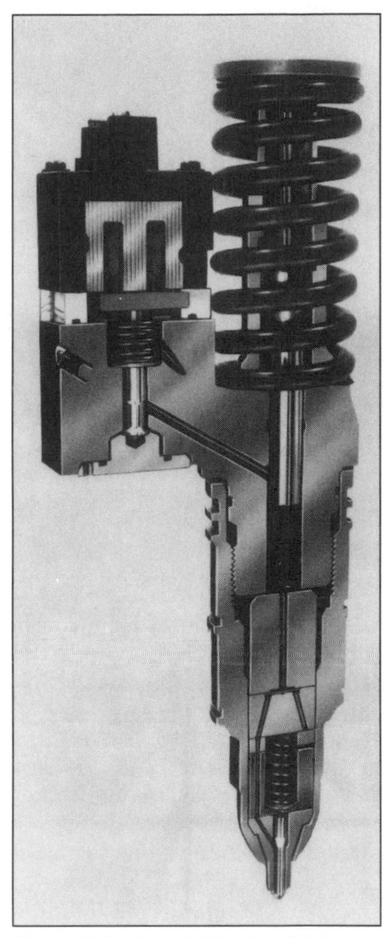

Figure 5-3 Detroit Diesel unit injector.

Each injector linkage is connected to the others by a **fuel rack**, so that all cylinders will disperse an identical amount of fuel at a given throttle setting. There are many advantages to the unit injector system: It requires fewer moving parts; it needs no high-pressure external fuel lines that could break or leak; and it is easier to troubleshoot, since each unit injector can easily be isolated, tested, and if need be, replaced. The principal disadvantage of the system is the need to precisely adjust the fuel rack so that each cylinder is "balanced" with the others.

Regardless of which kind of fuel system a diesel engine has, it's clear that the injection system must operate within extremely close tolerances and thus requires effective lubrication and cooling. Those functions are provided by the diesel fuel itself, more of which is pumped through the system than with the alternative, central injection pump design. To further cool fuel leaving the engine, some high-performance Detroit Diesels mount auxiliary heat exchangers.

The Governor

The amount of fuel the typical, carbureted gasoline engine ingests

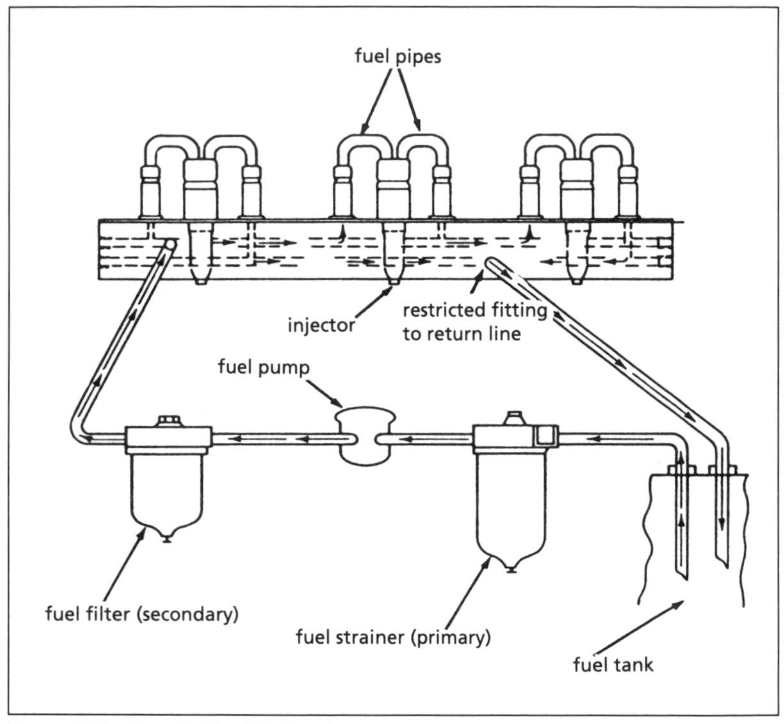

Figure 5-4 Detroit Diesel fuel rack.

is controlled by the amount of air rushing through the carburetor, which is in turn controlled by a butterfly valve. A diesel engine is designed to take in the same amount of air on each stroke regardless of the throttle setting, so some means must be found to prevent too much fuel from being injected into the combustion chambers before engine speed can handle it—for example, when a boat is idling along and the throttle is suddenly advanced. The mechanism that ensures that the ratio of fuel to air stays within relatively narrow prescribed bounds is the **governor**.

While many newer diesels are equipped with electronic governors, the mechanical type is more common. Usually this consists of a pair of weights that spin about an axis in direct proportion to engine speed. As engine speed increases, the weights spin faster and are thrown farther out by centrifugal force. Movement of the weights outward allows the injection pump or unit injectors to admit more fuel as the throttle is advanced. Thus in a typical diesel, the relationship between throttle setting and the amount of fuel injected into the engine is determined by engine speed, which is monitored by the governor.

The Cooling System

The cooling system of the typical marine diesel is not significantly different from that of the gasoline engine in your automobile, at least in its most basic form. To remove heat from various components, both engines circulate a supply of coolant within a closed loop via an engine-operated pump. The big difference is in how each type of engine removes heat from its coolant.

In your car, after the coolant leaves the engine it is circulated

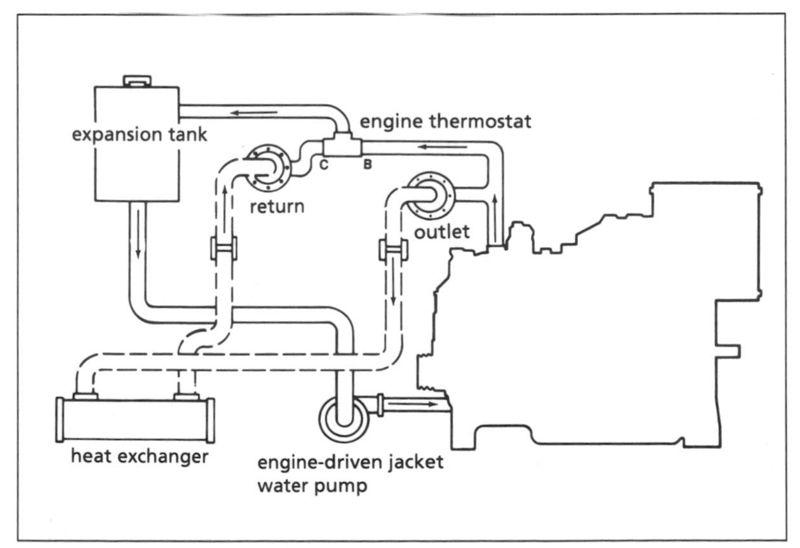

Figure 6-1 Typical cooling system.

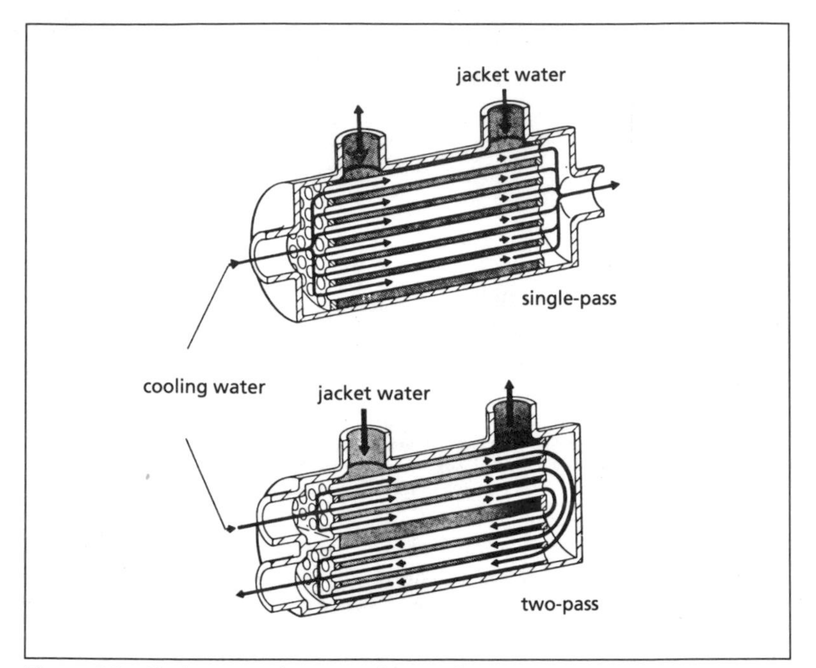

Figure 6-2 Single-pass and two-pass heat exchangers.

through an air-to-water heat exchanger, more commonly known as a **radiator**. Air passing over cooling fins attached to tubes containing the hot coolant carries away much of the heat in the same way that an intercooler reduces the temperature of air leaving a turbocharger.

In a boat, the heat exchanger is almost always the water-to-water type, in which the coolant-carrying tubes are surrounded not by air but by cooler raw water taken from outside the boat. Circulated by a second engine-driven pump, the raw water passes through a heat exchanger and is then pumped overboard, usually through the exhaust system. In most cases such a heat exchanger is clearly visible on the engine as a large cylinder with a large hose at either end (to allow raw water to enter and exit) and two smaller hoses on the sides (to allow coolant to enter and exit).

Additional Cooling

There are other differences between the cooling systems of the automotive gasoline engine and the marine diesel engine. For example, since oil is used for heat removal as well as for lubrication, the cooling system of the marine diesel must also accommodate an **oil cooler**, which is a second heat exchanger, usually smaller than the main unit. Often there is a third heat exchanger, typically either the same size as the oil cooler or slightly smaller, which cools the oil used in the hydraulic transmission.

In addition to all these burdens, the modern marine diesel cooling system often carries yet another. Today, most diesels are designed with the hottest components—the turbocharger's turbine side and the exhaust manifolds—enclosed in a water jacket to keep engine room temperatures down and reduce the chance of fire. A moderate engine room temperature is important not only for safety reasons, but also because—just as with the air leaving the turbocharger—when the air in the engine room gets hot it becomes less dense, and larger engines actually can "starve."

Another big difference in the cooling system of the marine diesel is that the surrounding water it must use for coolant often contains salt or impurities that make it corrosive to metallic components in general, and heat exchangers in particular. This requires the presence of some sort of corrosion protection system, which usually takes the form of a **zinc pencil**, or sacrificial zinc anode, that is inserted into the raw-water portion of the heat exchanger and is designed to corrode away before the unit's other metallic components.

Of the gasoline marine engines found on boats, at least half are raw-water cooled; that is, they simply take raw water and pump it through the block to cool the engine. The system has advantages—mainly simplicity and low cost—and disadvantages—mostly higher corrosion. Modern diesels must be freshwater cooled, as described above, with a closed coolant loop being in turn cooled by raw water circulated through a heat exchanger.

The reason is not so much one of corrosion, but rather one of temperature regulation. Unlike a gasoline engine that depends on a spark to ignite fuel, a diesel depends upon heat generated by compression. If the engine is allowed to fall below a certain temperature threshold, the heat of compression will be insufficient to effect complete combustion and poor fuel efficiency and high emissions levels will result. It is absolutely crucial that the diesel's temperature-regulating device—the **thermostat**—be left intact and operating for a diesel to run properly. A diesel that runs too cold is almost as bad as one that runs too hot.

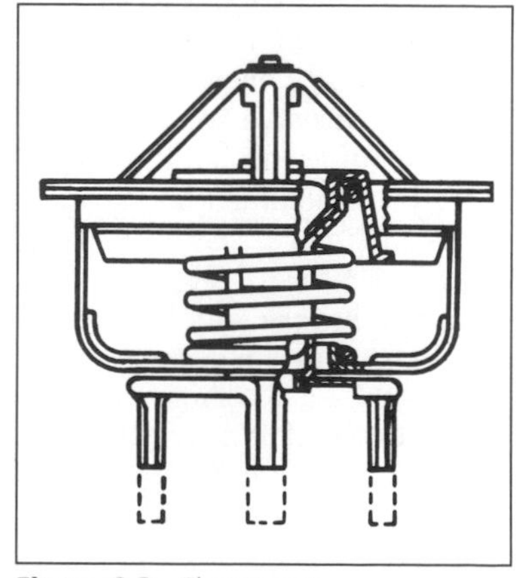

Figure 6-3 Thermostat.

The Lubrication System

The basic design of the diesel lubrication system differs little from that of your automobile. The differences are more of magnitude than of design. The primary components are a reservoir, or **oil sump**, an engine-driven **oil pump**, various passages that take the oil to components, and, of course, the oil itself.

Since diesel engine oil is called upon to do more work, typically there is more of it. A diesel engine may hold as much as four times more oil than a gasoline engine of comparable horsepower. Likewise, a diesel's oil filter usually is larger and thus more expensive. One final difference, as we've already seen, is that since the oil also functions as a coolant, some means must be provided for removing excess heat.

But the oil itself must be different, too. Diesel fuel often contains fairly significant amounts of sulfur which, after combustion, combine with naturally occurring moisture to produce sulfuric acid, an extremely corrosive compound. Diesel lubricating oil must be formulated to buffer this acidity, at least in the short term. It also must keep more particulate matter in suspension than oil designed for gasoline engines. Finally, diesel lubricating oil must cope with higher operating temperatures and pressures. For these reasons, diesel lubricating oil has to be specially formulated. Oil designed specifically for use in gasoline engines will cause immediate and significant damage if used in a diesel. Furthermore, turbocharged diesels demand oil with a special package of additives different from those suitable for non-turbocharged diesels. In Chapter 13 we'll discuss the American Petroleum Institute's classification system and how it relates to marine diesel engines.

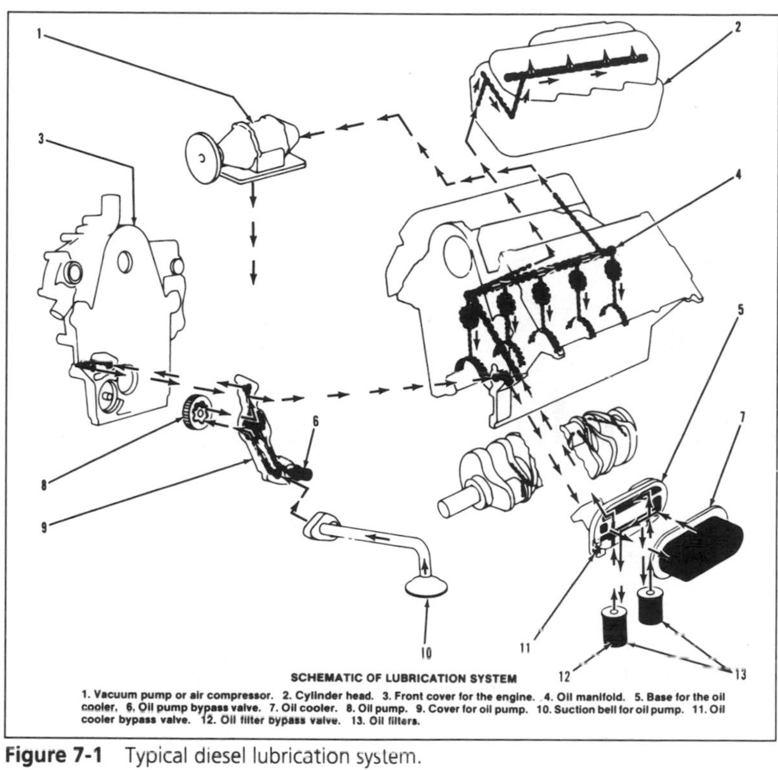

Figure 7-1 Typical diesel lubrication system.

The Exhaust System

On land, it's a relatively simple matter to dispose of diesel exhaust. After it leaves the cylinder head, it passes through a muffler to reduce the noise level, then it's vented into the atmosphere. Some commercial boats, where a high ambient noise level is not a concern, deal with diesel exhaust in a similar manner. These systems, usually called **dry stacks**, combine a muffler of sorts with a large, vertical pipe that ensures (at least in theory) that those on deck will not have to inhale diesel fumes. Such a system may work around commercial fishermen, but it is usually unacceptable on a pleasure boat where the owner has paid top dollar for a sleek appearance and demands at least a modicum of quiet.

As a result, the vast majority of noncommercial diesels use a variation of the water-cooled exhaust system. Water-cooling accomplishes two things: It reduces noise to acceptable levels, and it cools the ex-

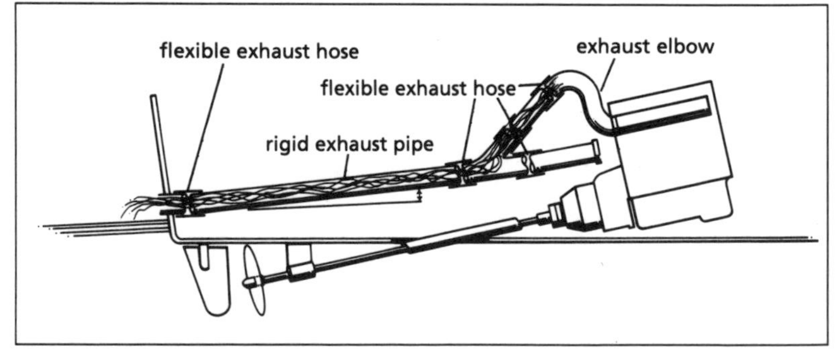

Figure 8-1 Wet exhaust system.

haust sufficiently to allow it to be routed safely through an interior pipe and out the transom.

The system is relatively simple. Exhaust leaves the combustion chamber and passes into an **exhaust manifold**, which usually is water-cooled. From here it passes to the **exhaust elbow**, a sort of reversed sink trap designed to ensure that water downstream of it cannot makes its way back into the cylinders. Since water does not compress, water in the combustion chamber results in **hydro-lock**, essentially freezing the engine.

One way water could possibly enter the combustion chamber is if the boat were suddenly accelerated in reverse, a fairly common practice in sportfishing called "backing down." In the absence of an exhaust elbow, the water could run back up the exhaust pipe, into the manifold and past an open valve, causing hydro-lock. Note, however, that in some large boats the diesel engines are already mounted high enough above the waterline to render exhaust elbows unnecessary.

Water Injection

At the elbow, or actually just after the highest point on the elbow, raw water is injected into the stream of exhaust. In most engines this is the same water that was pumped into the boat by the raw-water pump to cool the heat exchangers. (In boats that use a dry stack the raw water typically is pumped out through a separate through-hull fitting on the side of the boat.)

The exhaust elbow, where relatively cool water mixes with the hot

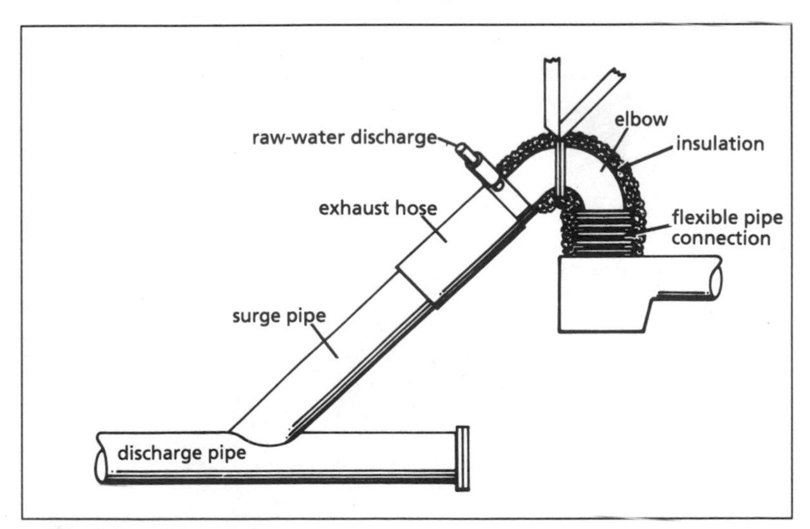

Figure 8-2 Exhaust elbow.

exhaust, is one of the hottest places in the exhaust system. Because the elbow is unprotected by sacrificial zincs, typically it is the point of highest corrosion on the engine. On most marine engines, the exhaust elbows are the first components that require replacement.

After the exhaust, now mixed with raw water, leaves the elbow, it may exit directly through the transom or, if greater acoustical damping is required, it may first pass through a muffler. A marine muffler is similar in design to its automotive counterpart but different in theory. The automotive muffler quiets exhaust by passing it through a series of baffles that break up the sonic waves in the gases. Marine mufflers also may use baffles, but they effect sound reduction by cooling the gases in pools of raw water, which also serves to dampen sound.

The Lift-Type Muffler

A similar marine unit is the **lift-type muffler**, a vertical canister that fills with water from the exhaust pipe until it reaches a sufficient level to overflow out a passage and out the exhaust. This pooling causes the gases to be diluted and cooled as they pass over the accumulated water, reducing sound. Lift-type mufflers are more common on smaller propulsion diesels and auxiliary generators.

Oddly enough, although they produce more horsepower and burn more fuel, turbocharged diesels typically have quieter exhausts than naturally aspirated models because the vanes of the turbine act as baffles, which breaks up the sonic waves and reduces noise.

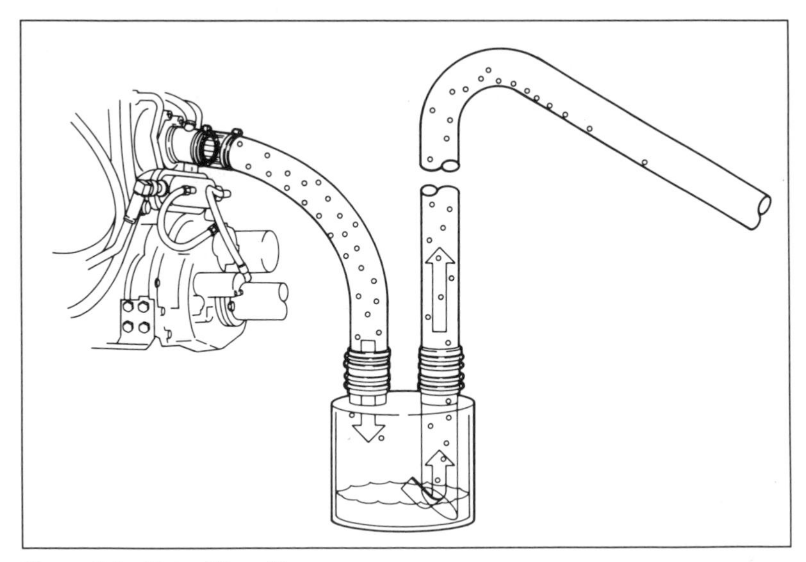

Figure 8-3 Water-lift muffler.

PART TWO

How to Operate a Marine Diesel Engine

The Log

The diesel engine is an amazingly reliable and durable piece of equipment. It powers everything from over-the-road trucks to earthmovers to continuous-duty generators and pumps. So it would seem that if it does so well in these commercial applications, it must hardly be taxed when installed in a pleasure boat.

It is true that in terms of gross operating hours, few noncommercial marine diesels will ever approach the kind of time racked up by commercial applications. But that doesn't necessarily mean their life is easier. Studies have shown repeatedly that the vast majority of wear in an internal combustion engine occurs at start-up, when the oil is cold and largely drained off most moving parts, and engine tolerances are less than they would be at operating temperatures. Professional diesel operators, whether on land or on water, follow certain guidelines to minimize this wear, guidelines that any boater should follow as well.

In the following two chapters you'll find two checklists; one should be referred to every time you take your boat out—no matter how short the trip. The other is a more involved periodic checklist that should be referred to every 30 days or so. The prudent boater not only will read and adhere to these checklists, but will post them in a conspicuous place so that he or she doesn't forget them in the rush to start a trip.

Where's the best place to post them? In the **log**. Yes, every boater who is serious about caring for and maintaining a diesel engine should have a log either dedicated to the engine and mechanical systems of the boat or to the overall boat itself. It need not be complicated—a simple spiral-bound notebook will do just fine—but it must contain certain information.

The following is a list of the basic data that should be entered into a log. Your log should be organized in chronological order, so you can quickly locate any event according to the time it occurred.

Record of Maintenance and Repairs

Being able to look at a single record and tell what has been maintained or repaired on your engine is a valuable asset. A proper record will detail the kind of work done, the date on which the work was done, the engine hour meter reading when the work was done, and the cost. It also will ensure that the next maintenance is done when it *should* be done. A proper log also should provide space for comments, both yours and particularly a mechanic's observations, perhaps regarding the cause of a specific problem or the likelihood of future problems.

It's important to note that there is only one yardstick by which to measure everything that happens to your diesel, and that's **engine hours**. There are some cases when a chronological interval (days or months) might dictate the need for work or maintenance, but it's far more likely that the determining factor will be the number of engine hours since the last service. If your boat is not equipped with an hour meter for each engine (including the generator's), either install one or have one installed immediately. The cost should not exceed $50 per engine and the benefit is well worth the price.

Record of Oil and Fuel Consumption

Adding a quart of oil is as forgettable an event as it is important. If you don't write it down, you'll never remember when you last added oil or how much you added. That means you'll have no idea how much oil your engine consumes over a period of time—the single most significant index to your engine's overall health.

Fuel consumption is the second most significant index of engine health. When fuel consumption increases, there must be a reason for it. It could be a heavier load, higher average operating speed, or even a faulty fuel system. Unless you have a fuel flow meter on board, you'll need to calculate your mileage by combining estimates of average speed, distance traveled, time underway, and fuel used, inferred from how much it takes to top off your tank. Do all your estimation in your logbook so you'll have a record of this data. Admittedly this will produce a less than totally precise figure; still it will be sufficiently accurate to be meaningful. If you're proficient at dead reckoning your position (getting a fix by estimating time, course, and speed), your estimation of total fuel consumption is likely to be fairly accurate.

Gauge Readings

You should make note of the readings of your most important

gauges at start-up, once the engine has reached operating speed, and just before it is shut down. Among the parameters you will want to make note of are idle speed, engine oil pressure, engine oil temperature (before and after warm-up), coolant temperature, exhaust temperature (after warm-up), and even battery voltage. If your transmission has gauges that register its oil temperature and pressure, note these.

Obviously, you can carry this kind of thing so far that you'll never leave the dock, but even a complete inventory should take no more than a couple of minutes. To save space, use shorthand. For instance, if your diesel produces 60 pounds of oil pressure when cold and 40 pounds when hot, you could write it thus: oil: 60 lb.-C/40 lb.-H.

The purpose of all this is to establish an operating baseline, a list of criteria that you can point to as constituting the typical operating characteristics of your engine. This can be particularly valuable when you have to call a mechanic, but it also can be valuable when you refer to it by establishing an operational trend. For instance, if you looked at your log over the last 100 hours and noted that at the beginning your engine typically operated at 180°F and today it is running at 195°F, you'd have reason to be concerned. Assuming the engine's load or operating speed hasn't changed drastically, you'd have to suspect the possibility of a cooling system problem, even though the temperature may not be hot enough to trigger an engine alarm.

Noting operating trends is your biggest weapon in the fight to avoid costly repair bills. Most engines do not simply break down; they usually degrade over time and, when they do, they leave a fairly clear trail of clues pointing to their problem.

Observations

As we will see in subsequent chapters, you can tell a great deal about the state of your engine by observing certain physical signs, such as the color of its exhaust, the smoothness with which it idles and runs, how easy or difficult it is to start, the presence of any oil in the bilge, and yes, even the noises it makes. After you've spent many hours at the wheel you'll probably develop a certain "feel" for your engine, just as commercial boaters do, and you'll know when something just doesn't seem right. Whatever observations you make about the way your diesel operates are important, if not at the moment, then as indicators of trends. Write them down; some day they may come in handy.

Ambient Temperature and Humidity

All the notations above can't be properly interpreted unless you know the ambient (outside your boat) conditions. Why? Because both temperature and humidity have a direct effect on how your engine operates. If you don't know how cold it was when you noted that the diesel was difficult to start, the observation is largely useless. Likewise, if you can't see that when your engine was operating at 190°F you were in the Bahamas and the water temperature was 88°F, that observation may have little meaning.

How do you get such information? The easiest way is simply to turn your VHF to its weather channel (which you should do before you start any day aboard a boat) and listen to the NOAA reports, which will in time give you the current air temperature and humidity.

All things being equal, the higher the ambient temperature, the less horsepower your diesel will produce, since hot air is less dense, allowing less oxygen to reach the combustion chamber per stroke. Conversely, the higher the humidity, the more horsepower your diesel will produce, since high humidity readings indicate more water in the air, and water contains one molecule of oxygen for every two of hydrogen.

On most NOAA weather broadcasts, you'll also be able to learn the temperature of the surrounding water. This is just as important to interpreting your readings as air temperature and humidity. The cooler the outside water, the more efficiently your engine's heat exchangers will work, and the cooler (within limits) your engine coolant and oil and your transmission oil will be.

Again, this information can be acquired painlessly and jotted down quickly in shorthand. If the air temperature is 90°F, the humidity is 80 percent, and the water temperature is 86°F, you can write it quickly as AT90/H80/WT86. Then you can close up your logbook and go outside, because you're probably in the Bahamas.

Maintenance and Repair Log

Date	Work Done	Engine Hours	Cost	Comments
9/10/89	—	4280-91	—	passage from St. Lucie to Miami
9/12/89	oil change	4291	$ 112.60	Steven's Marina
9/16/89	—	4292-97	—	passage to Islamorada noted black smoke
9/17/89	fuel rack ADJ	4297	$ 169.50	to correct over-fueling
9/21/89	—	4297-99	—	passage to Key South
9/22/89	fuel-up	4299	$ 999.21	662 gas, 490 miles 0.79 mpg
9/27/89	—	4300-18	—	passage from Key South to Key West
9/29/89	top off oil	4318	$ 6.10	down two quarts
9/30/89	oil analysis	4318	$ 29.00	all ok, see att. report

Figure 9-1 Sample Logs (continued on following pages)

Daily Engine Log					
Date	9/10/89				
Hours	11 (2010)				
Oil Added	none				
Fuel Consumption	approx. 190 gal				
Gauges at startup					
RPM	Oil Pressure	Oil Temp.	Coolant	Exhaust Temp.	Voltage
750	40	175	175	190	14.0
Observations					
everything normal					

Daily Engine Log					
Date	9/11/89				
Hours	4 (2014)				
Oil Added	none				
Fuel Consumption	approx. 120 gal				
Gauges at startup					
RPM	Oil Pressure	Oil Temp.	Coolant	Exhaust Temp.	Voltage
750	40	175	180	190	14.0
Observations					
black smoke underway					

Daily Engine Log					
Date	9/12/89				
Hours	4 (2018)				
Oil Added	one quart				
Fuel Consumption	approx. 65 gal				
Gauges at startup					
RPM	Oil Pressure	Oil Temp.	Coolant	Exhaust Temp.	Voltage
750	40	180	190	190	14.0
Observations					
black smoke; oil & coolant temps higher					

Daily Engine Log					
Date	9/13/89				
Hours	5 (2023)				
Oil Added	none				
Fuel Consumption	fill up — 490 gal since 2014				
Gauges at startup					
RPM	Oil Pressure	Oil Temp.	Coolant	Exhaust Temp.	Voltage
750	40	190	200	190	14.0
Observations					
black smoke; oil &coolant temps higher since 9/11/90					

Daily Engine Log					
Date	9/14/89				
Hours	4 (2037)				
Oil Added	none				
Fuel Consumption	approx. 35 gal				
Gauges at startup					
RPM	Oil Pressure	Oil Temp.	Coolant	Exhaust Temp.	Voltage
750	40	190	200	190	14.0
Observations					
smoke normal (rack re-adjusted) — temps still high					

Daily Engine Log					
Date	9/15/89				
Hours	5 (2042)				
Oil Added	none				
Fuel Consumption	approx. 41 gal				
Gauges at startup					
RPM	Oil Pressure	Oil Temp.	Coolant	Exhaust Temp.	Voltage
750	40	175	175	190	14.0
Observations					
temps normal — through-hull fitting cleaned out					

The Daily Checklist

Yes, it's a pain. You'd much rather just fire up that diesel and head off into the sunrise. You've dealt with enough hassles during the week; now's the time to relax. But don't. Just take a few minutes—that's all it will take—to make a few crucial checks. Those few minutes are essential to your preventative maintenance program. They will help ensure that your trip really will be hassle-free. Make yourself a short checklist, including the following items, and post it in a prominent place so you don't forget.

Check Your Oil

You may have done it just yesterday, but do it again today and every morning before you take off. It is entirely possible that during the last eight hours of running something went wrong—maybe your mechanic forgot to tighten the oil filter—and you're down to your last few quarts of oil. Just two or three more hours of running and that oil pump will start sucking air, and there you go: burned bearings, busted trip, and *big* repair dollars.

Just pull the dip stick, wipe it off with a clean cloth, punch it back in, and note its reading. Then stop for a moment and think: Is it significantly lower than yesterday? If so, make a note of it in your log. Perhaps today you'll want to check it again at midday when you drop the hook for lunch, just to see if it's gotten any worse. Just remember to wait about 10 minutes between shutdown and checking to allow most of the oil to drain back into the oil pan. Otherwise you'll get an erroneously low reading on your dip stick.

If you've been keeping a log, you know where your engine oil level normally runs on the dip stick. If you haven't, it may fool you. For some reason—no one seems to know why—some engines simply will not run at the full mark on the stick. If that's the case with your diesel, make a note of it in your log. If it's a chronic operating condition (and you're sure it is), you may want to go so far as scratching a second full mark on the dip stick to signify the "normal" operating level.

In many marine installations the engine must be tilted to accommodate the propeller shaft angle. Unfortunately, the engine builder graduates the dip stick assuming the engine will be mounted level, so these factory marks could be either high or low. The boatbuilder is supposed to re-mark the dip stick to the actual normal operating level, but sometimes this isn't done.

If that's the case with your engine, you may be constantly adding oil in a futile effort to keep the level at the top mark while your engine is happily blowing the excess away. If you've kept note of all this in your log, you'll probably note something is awry and re-mark your dip stick, or at the very least stop adding oil. If you don't keep a log, you'll probably just keep pouring oil in the engine and cursing the engine builder who put together such a sloppy piece of machinery.

Check Coolant Level

The proper amount of coolant is crucial to the health of your diesel. If it drops significantly, the circulating pump will begin to suck air, causing bubbles to form. Each bubble will become a hot spot, and eventually your diesel will overheat.

In the world of engines, one of the greatest inventions is also one of the simplest: the coolant recovery bottle. Today, most engines are equipped with this simple, translucent plastic container that tells visually, without ever removing a cap, the level of coolant in the engine. If your engine doesn't have a coolant recovery bottle either purchase one and install it yourself or have your mechanic install one. With it in place, all you need do is cast a glance toward the bottle and note whether the level falls somewhere between the "high" and "low" marks. If it does, your job is done.

If it doesn't, top it off and note the fact in your log. Too much topping off indicates either a leak or an engine that is overheating—and maybe a boater who isn't watching the temperature gauge (it also could mean a faulty gauge).

Whatever the case, when you top off make sure you add the same type of coolant that is already in the engine. Typically, this is a mixture of half antifreeze and half water, but your engine may be different. Be aware of what is in the system, make up a gallon container of it, and keep it on hand so you can keep the level where it should be. If you or your mechanic has added a rust preventative to the cooling system, be aware that it will be diluted each time you top off. Refer to your log and when necessary add more product.

As with oil, some engines seem to prefer a certain level of coolant that may not fall within the two marks on the coolant bottle. After you've made certain there is no problem, make a note of this fact in your log and don't try to keep the bottle topped off. The coolant will only overflow into the bilge, be pumped out, and pollute the surrounding water. The best solution is simply to re-mark the bottle with levels that your engine can live with.

If your engine has no coolant bottle and you choose not to install one, you'll have to remove the cap to check the fluid level. If you do this daily in the morning before you start up, there'll be no problem because your engine will be stone cold. If it isn't, **use extreme caution when removing the cap**. Even an engine that has been shut down for a couple of hours may still have a pressurized cooling system due to an elevated temperature and concomitant coolant expansion. Not only can pressurized engine coolant burn you, it is also a toxic substance that can, among other things, damage your eyes. To be safe, only check an engine that has sat overnight.

If you're checking your coolant by removing the cap, note than most systems are not designed to be filled to the rim. Check your owner's manual and chances are you'll find that the proper cold level is somewhere from one to two inches below the rim. Stick your finger in; if it comes out wet, everything is okay.

One final note about coolant checks: Observe the color of the coolant. Today's antifreezes come in various colors, but you should be alert for any unusual cloudiness or pink coloration that may signal incipient corrosion. By checking your log you should know your engine coolant's "normal" color. If there's any significant variance, it may mean that the system should be flushed and filled with new coolant.

Check the Transmission Oil Level

Just as important to the reliability of your boat is the condition of your transmission. You should be able to locate its dip stick easily (it's on the inboard side where you can reach it). Use the same procedures that you use in checking your engine's oil level.

Check Your Battery's Electrolyte Level

If your batteries are difficult to locate this can be a real task. You may have to resort to a mirror and flashlight to get a good reading, but even if you must, don't skip this checkpoint. Make sure you know what the proper electrolyte level is; too much can be as bad as too little. A good rule of thumb is that the level should be about halfway between the plates and the top of the battery. And while you're there, check to ensure that the battery is securely mounted, that there is no sign of fluid around it (an indication of a cracked battery case), and that the terminals are not corroded or dirty. Be careful; battery electrolyte is an acid that can harm you and your boat.

Conduct a General Visual Survey of the Engine

Before you consider your job finished, take a quick look around for signs of trouble, perhaps a pool of oil or coolant, missing paint, or something loose. Grab some of the external components and shake them to make sure they're secure. Look under the engine, not only for leakage but also for errant bolts and nuts.

If your engine is equipped with a fuel/water separator (we'll explain it in Chapter 14), you should also visually check its transparent bowl for discoloration due to contamination by water or dirt. At the same time, check the sea-water strainer (if so equipped) for the presence of weeds or other material.

Log It

Write down the results of your checks in your log, even if everything is normal. Just knowing precisely when it was that you last checked over your engine and precisely what you did can be a valuable advantage in the battle to keep your boat running smoothly.

The Daily Checklist: A Summary

❑ **Oil**	Wait at least 10 minutes after shutdown; check log to determine trends.
❑ **Coolant**	If engine is equipped with recovery bottle, check level visually. If engine has no recovery bottle, wait until engine has cooled, preferably overnight, before removing coolant cap to check. Look for discoloration. Be sure to add type and mixture of coolant already in the engine.
❑ **Transmission Oil**	Add only the recommended oil.
❑ **Battery**	Check electrolyte level, mountings, and for signs of leaking.
❑ **General**	Look for oil or coolant leaks, loose parts, parts in the drip pan, frayed belts, soft hoses, or anything out of the ordinary.
❑ **Log**	Whatever action you take, note it in the log.

11

The Periodic Check

For day-to-day operation, the simple daily check specified in the previous chapter is sufficient, but every 30 days or 20 hours of engine time, you should plan to spend a little more time in the engine room, checking things with a closer eye. Again, even this more thorough perusal should take only a little of your time—maybe 20 minutes.

Before you start, you'll need a few simple tools. One of the most important is a flashlight, preferably one that throws a small, high-intensity beam. Also important are a rubber-tipped hammer, a flat-blade screwdriver, and an adjustable wrench.

Periodic checks are best conducted when the engine has sat idle overnight, because you'll be crawling around and touching many of the components, which will be hot if the engine's been running. Likewise, you'll probably want to wear either a pair of coveralls or at least some old clothing. And finally, bring along a note pad, or better yet, your logbook, so you can record your observations.

Examine the Oil

The first step in the periodic check is to conduct the five-point daily checklist referred to in the previous chapter. However, this time when you check your oil you'll want to take the time to observe it more closely for signs of coolant contamination. Any liquid in oil usually shows up as an iridescence in strong light, so your flashlight will come in handy here.

You cannot determine how clean or dirty your oil is by looking at it, because today's high-detergent oils are designed to turn black almost immediately after use. The only way to really determine the condition of your oil is to draw a sample of it and send it out for an **oil analysis**.

Jordan-Milton CAT

Jordan-Milton Machinery Inc.

JORDAN MILTON MACHINERY INC
MARINE ENGINE DIVISION
EXIT 7 INTERSTATE 89
WARNER, N.H. 03278
1-603-746-4671

SCHEDULED OIL SAMPLING
WEAR ANALYSIS

MAKE	MODEL	SERIAL NUMBER	JOB SITE
CAT	3412	60MXXXXX	MARINE ENGINE

OWNER UNIT NO.	COMPARTMENT
MAINE	DIESEL ENGINE

WEAR METALS ARE REPORTED IN PARTS PER MILLION — PHYSICAL TESTS — INFRARED

LAB CONTROL NUMBER	BOTTLE LABEL	DATE SAMPLE TAKEN	DATE SAMPLE PROCESSED	MAKE UP OF OIL ADDED IN QUARTS	HOURS MILES ON UNIT	HOURS MILES ON OIL	OIL CHANGED?	COPPER CU	IRON FE	CHROMIUM CR	ALUMINUM AL	SILICON SI	LEAD PB		SODIUM NA			FUEL DILUTION	ANTI FREEZE	WATER	VISCOSITY	SOOT		
25775	15026	1/31/89	2/01/89	80.0	15325	250	Y	9	21	1	3	10	7	1	12			N	N	N		56	27	43
WEAR RATES LOOK GOOD AFTER MAJOR OVERHAUL NO PROBLEMS INDICATED AT THIS TIME RESAMPLE AT NORMAL INTERVAL																								
25099	15027	1/10/89	1/20/89	.0	UNKNWN	450	Y	20	39	1	8	8	13	1	12			N	N	N		76	20	37
WEAR RATES GREATLY IMPROVED THIS SAMPLE WERE THERE REPAIRS MADE ON THIS ENGINE? RESAMPLE NORMAL DRAIN TO CONTINUE MONITORING																								
24112	15021	12/30/88	1/05/89	.0			N	43	228	6	39	11	67	1	18			N	N	N		128	80	133
LEAD, IRON, ALUMINUM AND SOOT UNACCEPTABLE/URGENT RECOMMEND INSPECT & CORRECT AS NECESSARY CHANGE OIL AFTER REPAIRS & RESAMPLE NORMAL DRAIN																								
20981	15023	11/10/88	11/14/88	32.0	15205	205	N	4	35	1	3	10	8	3	15			N	N	N		102	50	100
ALL LEVELS ACCEPTABLE NO PROBLEMS INDICATED AT THIS TIME RESAMPLE AT NORMAL INTERVAL																								
20025	13464	10/24/88	10/27/88	.0	15000	164	Y	3	31	1	1	11	8	1	11			N	N	N		70	30	57
ALL LEVELS ACCEPTABLE NO PROBLEMS INDICATED AT THIS TIME RESAMPLE AT NORMAL INTERVAL																								
12622	13461	7/11/88	7/12/88	16.0	13637	324	Y	4	22	1	3	6	7	1	17			N	N	N		58	27	50
ALL LEVELS ACCEPTABLE NO PROBLEMS INDICATED AT THIS TIME RESAMPLE AT NORMAL INTERVAL																								

Figure 11-1 Most diesel shops can analyze your oil and provide you with advance notice of engine problems and an accurate estimation of your engine's condition.

Analysis is available from a variety of laboratories (usually listed in the Yellow Pages under "Laboratories, Spectrographic") or from a local engine repair facility.

You should have your engine's oil analyzed every three months or 50 engine hours. The report you receive will tell you in easy-to-understand language everything from how fast your engine is wearing to whether it's blown a head gasket. Best of all, oil analysis is cheap, usually around $12 per test.

Test the Coolant

You'll also be checking your coolant as part of your daily test, but this time you'll need a **coolant tester**, an inexpensive (less than $10) syringe-like device that tells at a glance the concentration of antifreeze in your engine's cooling system. Antifreeze contains rust inhibitors that are crucial to your engine's health, but the effectiveness of these and all the additives in antifreeze will degrade over time, eventually leaving your engine unprotected. An antifreeze tester is the only way you can check the potency of your engine coolant. If the reading falls below the recommended minimum, top off with some fresh coolant.

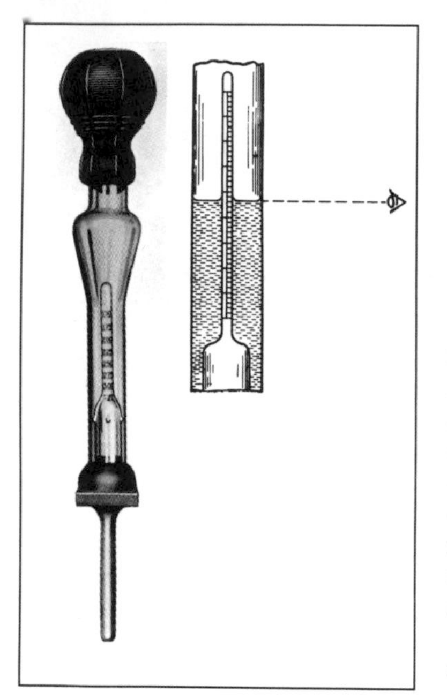

Figure 11-2 A battery-testing hydrometer, and its close cousin, the coolant tester, can paint an accurate portrait of your battery's state of charge (or your coolant's level of protection) at a glance—for less than $10.

Check Your Battery's State of Charge

You'll be checking the fluid level in your battery again, but this time you'll be more thorough. The syringe-like **hydrometer**, which will indicate the state of charge in each battery cell, is the tool of choice here. This is important because your battery may read 12 volts or higher on a voltmeter and yet one cell may be significantly weaker than the others, pointing toward trouble down the road. Even the best hydrometers (those that compensate for temperature) won't exceed $20 and are simple to use. Keep one on board.

Check the Plumbing

At this point you'll begin a more thorough check of your engine. The first things you should check are hoses and clamps. Squeeze the hoses. A good hose should be firm and resilient; one that has broken down will feel mushy and collapse easily under pressure; it should be replaced. Also, use your flashlight to look for signs of peeling, cracking, or other external indications of breakdown.

Test clamps with your screwdriver to ensure they're tight. If you find one that isn't, tighten it, but be careful: these clamps strip easily. As a safety measure, all hoses, especially those carrying raw water, should be double-clamped. Don't forget to check all through-hull fittings for leaks and signs of wear. Open and close all sea cocks to ensure they work easily. Note that some types have Zerk-style grease fittings and require lubrication with a grease gun about every 90 days.

Check the Electrical System

Next check all electrical wiring, with special attention given terminals and connections. Check for loose spots by pulling gently on the wire—you'd rather have it come apart here than somewhere out in the ocean. Temporary repairs can be effected with twist connectors and electrician's tape, but permanent repairs should be done with clamp-style electrical connectors or solder, and be covered with heat-sensitive shrink wrap.

Selectively tighten terminals with your screwdriver. Look for dangling wires and support them at closely spaced intervals either with tape or with tie-wraps. Note signs of chafing where wiring passes through bulkheads or metal components. Any loss of insulation, even if the wire isn't exposed, demands repair and preventative measures to see that it doesn't get worse.

Check the Hard and Soft Lines

Next, turn your attention toward the fuel lines. Most fuel passages on today's diesels are either internal or "hard lines"; that is, they are metal, usually copper. Hard lines demand little more than a visual check for leaks at joints. But to allow the engine to move on its mounts, all engines must have at least one run of "soft" lines, made of rubber or synthetic. Check soft lines carefully for signs of abrasion by grasping them and running your hand down their length. Any deep cuts or abrasions mean the hose should be replaced, *not* repaired. Also look here for signs of "weeping" at connection points.

Besides your inventory of coolant lines, you'll also want to check other clamped soft lines for integrity. These may include those carrying air from the turbocharger (if so equipped) or air cleaner (if so equipped) to the intake manifold. Just as diesels need soft fuel lines to accommodate movement, they also require soft exhaust lines. Give these a quick visual check and tighten their clamps if necessary.

Check Your Engine's Physical Condition

One other stop on your visual inventory is the engine mounts. Look for any signs of looseness and be especially watchful for cracks developing around the fiberglass in the way of the engine mounts. Rap them a few times with your rubber hammer to ensure they're solid.

Next check over your engine's principal components to make sure they're all tight. These may include the heat exchanger, intake and exhaust manifolds, alternator, raw-water pump, and turbocharger. This is also a good time to check the V-belts, looking for signs of **glazing** (a slick, polished appearance on the inside of the belt) due to slippage and cracks, and fraying on the outside usually because of aging. A good rule of thumb for belt tightness is that you shouldn't be able to deflect the belt more than 1/2 inch. If you can, the belt needs tightening. But don't over-tighten; that will place excessive strain on alternator and water-pump bearings.

Less frequently—about every 90 days—remove the zinc pencils from each of your heat exchangers and see how much of each is left.

Remember, these are supposed to wear away, but if they get much below half gone you should replace them. Don't be alarmed if some water spurts out of the hole left when you remove the zinc. Just have a spare on hand to replace it if need be.

Make a thorough inspection of all the areas where engine components are attached, looking for signs of leakage. In some engines, a certain amount of oil weepage is normal. Wipe it off, note it in your logbook, and check it again next time. One spot where you commonly may find weepage is around the breather cap on top of the valve cover. Again, some is normal; too much may be a sign of trouble. Also note that the vent itself often requires periodic cleaning in a solvent. If your engine is a V, look in the valley between the cylinder banks. Any significant pooling of coolant or oil should be noted. And don't forget to look under the engine as well.

Clean Up

Leave your engine and engine room as clean and free of oil and grease as possible. A clean environment makes it easier to spot oil or coolant leaks. Likewise, touch up any chipped paint or bare metal with an approved paint designed to withstand high temperatures. Not only will it make your engine look nicer, it also will help resist corrosion and make real problems easier to spot.

The Periodic Checklist: A Summary

- ❑ **Oil** — Check level; send out sample for analysis.
- ❑ **Coolant** — Check level; check potency with coolant tester.
- ❑ **Battery** — Check electrolyte level, mountings, leakage, and state of charge in each cell with a hydrometer.
- ❑ **Hoses** — Look for leaks or deterioration (hoses should be firm, not mushy); check for loose or corroded clamps.
- ❑ **Electrical** — Test for loose terminals; check for sealed connections; look for frayed wiring and worn insulation.
- ❑ **Fuel Lines** — Check hard lines; look for abrasion on soft lines; look for weeping at connections.
- ❑ **Soft Lines** — Check all clamped lines for tightness and integrity.

❑ **Engine Mounts**	Look for signs of looseness; look for cracks in fiberglass mounting points.
❑ **Miscellaneous**	Check for tightness of heat exchanger, intake manifold, exhaust manifold, alternator, raw water pump, and turbocharger.
❑ **V-Belts**	Look for fraying or glazing; check for proper tightness (1/2 inch of play).
❑ **Zincs**	Replace any that are more than half gone.
❑ **Leaks**	Check the drip pan, vents, hoses and lines, gaskets, all mating surfaces, cylinder valley (V-engines).
❑ **Log**	Note anything out of the ordinary in your log.

From Start-Up to Shutdown

The few minutes immediately after a diesel is started and just before it is shut down are the most crucial times in the engine's life. They will, in large part, determine how long your diesel will last.

Start-Up

After you've completed your preliminary checks, you're ready to start your diesel. You'll notice that many captains "pump" the throttle a few times to "prime" the engine before turning the key. Although it may look authoritative, it is a waste of time and actually may make the engine harder to start by overfueling it. Remember that the diesel depends not upon an electrical spark to initiate combustion but upon the heat generated by compression. In a cold engine, each piston may have to travel up and down the cylinder a couple of times before the combustion chamber is really hot. In other words, you'll probably have to crank a cold diesel a good deal longer than you would a cold gasoline engine before it fires off. This is normal; be patient and don't resort to pumping the throttle madly.

Once the engine starts, keep the r.p.m. level low for at least 90 seconds. The boater who fires up his diesel and then "revs" it up like a teenage street racer is surely grinding away precious engine life because he hasn't allowed the minute or two necessary for oil to begin fully circulating. A good guideline is to set the throttle just above idle and leave it there, generating no more that 1,000 r.p.m. Once the engine starts, you can leave the helm to conduct various chores such as pulling in fenders and dock lines; by the time you come back, your engine will be ready to run.

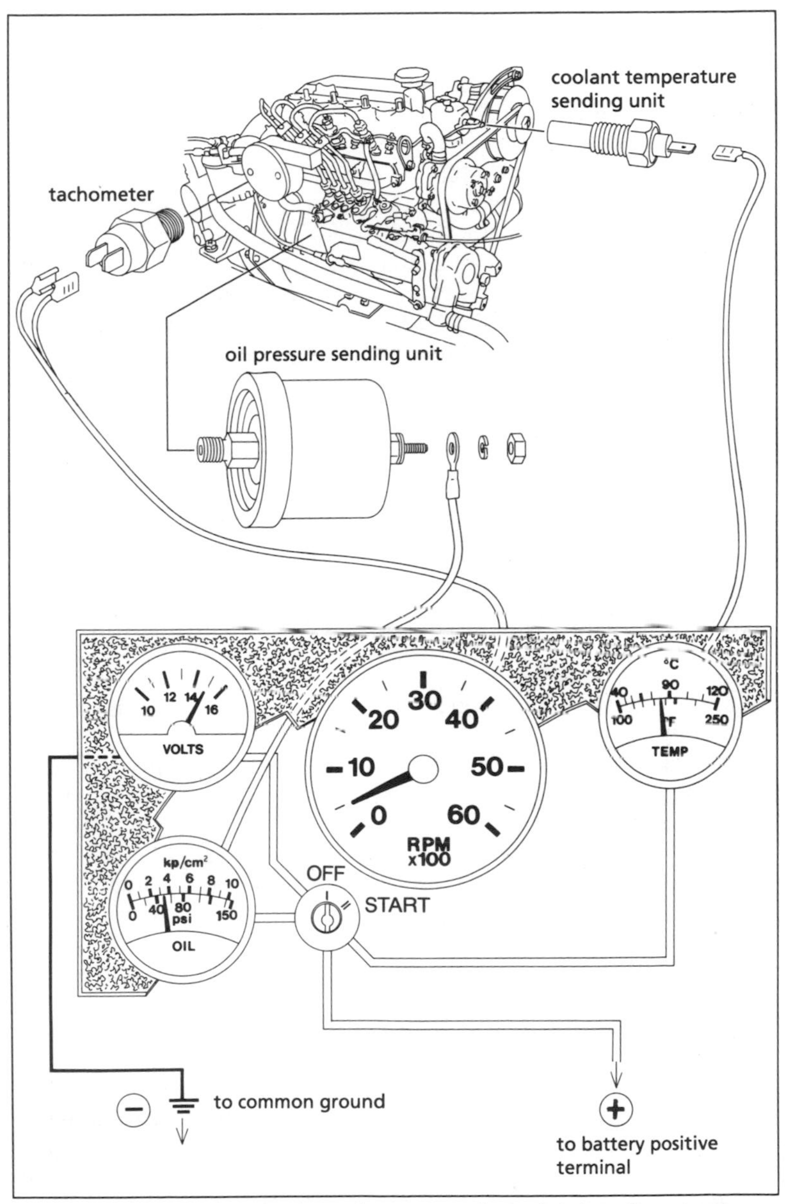

Figure 12-1 Gauges constantly monitor your engine's vital signs. If you log the normal readings at idle and cruising speed, you'll be able to spot problems as they happen, before they can cause serious damage.

Shoving Off

Once you've let the engine idle for 90 seconds or so, you're ready to shove off. But that doesn't mean the diesel is fully warmed up. You can tell when a gasoline engine is warmed up by looking at the temperature gauge, which measures the engine coolant's temperature. When it rises into the designated area, the engine is at operating temperature.

Diesels have coolant temperature gauges too, but they are not good indicators of when an engine is at operating temperature. The best indicator of diesel engine operating temperature is an **oil temperature gauge**. That's because a diesel engine has a thermostat in its cooling system that prevents coolant from reaching the heat exchanger if the engine isn't producing sufficient heat. Most gasoline engines also have a thermostat, but the difference is that eventually they can generate sufficient heat to open the thermostat without being under load. A diesel engine is more load-sensitive and usually will not warm up unless it is performing work.

Consequently, you may be idling out a channel for half an hour, yet your temperature gauge may not budge. But all the time oil is circulating throughout the engine, lubricating and cooling, and the engine actually is ready to go to work. The reverse also can be true: engine coolant temperature can be high enough to indicate it is warm but the oil may not have warmed sufficiently to fully lubricate the engine. The engine still isn't ready to work. Obviously, if your engine doesn't have an oil temperature gauge, you should have one installed—and use it.

Once you're certain the engine is ready to go to work—by whatever means—you can apply a load. You can, if you insist, simply shove the throttles all the way forward and wait for the engine to come up to the desired speed. The governor will ensure that the proper amount of fuel will be added only when the engine speed can handle it.

But the prudent captain applies the throttles slowly and gradually, knowing that a smooth application of power reduces overall engine load and stress while getting the boat to the desired speed nearly as quickly. This method also saves fuel, since you don't have to throttle back to cruising speed.

Choosing a Cruising Speed

The next question is at what speed you should cruise a diesel. It is widely accepted that the average diesel can cruise safely at a higher percentage of its full-throttle operating speed than a gasoline engine. A widely circulated rule of thumb states that you can cruise most diesels at about 200 to 400 r.p.m. below the peak operating speed.

In deciding where you want to cruise, you may also want to balance other factors as well. For instance, the faster an engine—any engine—turns the higher the wear rate. In other words, an engine turning

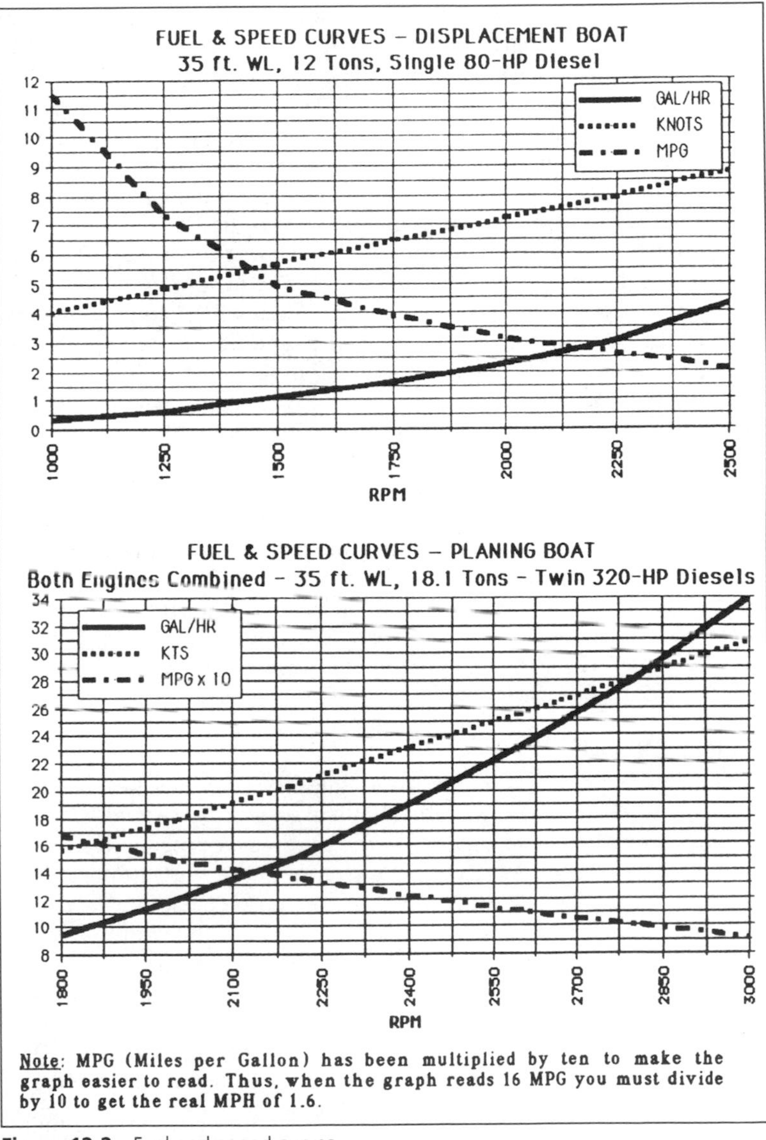

Figure 12-2 Fuel and speed curves.

at an average speed of 2,200 r.p.m. will wear faster than an identical engine that turns at an average speed of 1,800 r.p.m. Note that this is not a direct relationship; increasing speed 10 percent does not necessarily increase wear rates by 10 percent.

Wear rates are a function not only of engine operating speed, but of load as well, and in marine engines, load is determined, at least in part, by hull characteristics. Typically, displacement hulls require less horsepower (producing less load) to drive them at slower speeds, yet absorb more power (higher loads) at higher engine speeds without producing a directly proportional increase in motion speed. The efficiency of planing hulls, on average, peaks later in the r.p.m. scale and then falls off as the engine approaches full throttle.

Optimum fuel efficiency varies with each combination of hull, engine, reduction ratio, propeller, and load. The only way to determine the most efficient speed at which to cruise is either to test the boat yourself in its final trim with a fuel flowmeter or accept the figures published by any number of magazines that test boats.

If you're looking for some very rough guidelines, however, here are two: For displacement hulls, run the engine about 200 to 400 r.p.m. below planing speed. (You'll be able to tell when you reach the planing threshold because boat speed will stop increasing as quickly when you advance the throttle.) Those who own planing hulls can assume that best cruise will occur about 400 to 600 r.p.m. after the boat reaches plane. This is because such speeds allow most hulls to generate a little more speed and really break free of the water, yet remain relatively unaffected by the increasing resistance of higher speeds. Of course, if you're in no hurry and can afford to be conservative, you can use this rule: The slower you go, the easier on the engine.

Shutting Down

The rule here is simple, but often ignored: **Give the diesel time to cool down before shutting it off.** This is particularly crucial with turbocharged engines, where the turbine/compressor bearing needs time to cool. The most prudent course is to reverse the start-up procedure. Pull into the dock or mooring, throttle the engine back to idle, and go about your anchoring/mooring chores for three or four minutes while your engine cools down. Then you can safely shut it off.

Many boaters with turbocharged engines follow this procedure only to commit one fatal error. They can't resist that last punch of the throttle to rev up the engine before switching off the key. When they do, they typically spool the turbocharger up to between 30,000 and 40,000 r.p.m., then shut the engine off, stopping the supply of oil to the compressor/turbine bearing. The engine stops but the turbine continues to spin for another 30 seconds, baking the oil left on the shaft and causing severe scoring of the shaft and bearing.

Moral: Once you've taken the time to let the diesel cool down, resist the urge to blip the throttle; simply turn off the key.

PART THREE

How to Care for Your Marine Diesel Engine

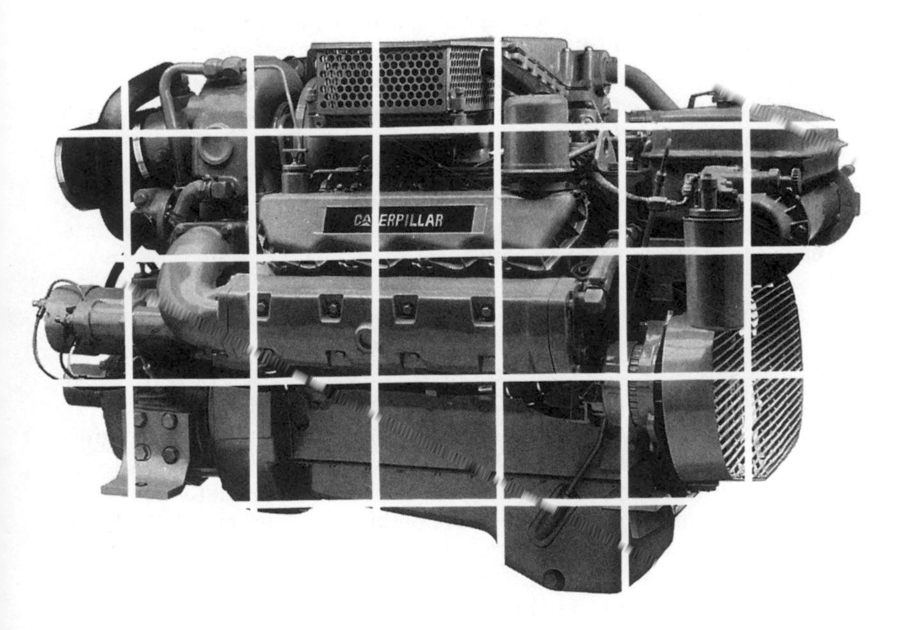

Caring for Oil

This chapter is not meant to contradict in any way the maintenance schedule and manufacturer's recommendations included in your owner's manual. On the contrary, it is complementary and is intended to help you better fulfill those guidelines.

One of the beauties of the diesel engine is that it is a relatively low-maintenance piece of machinery. Compared to the gasoline engine, it lacks a complex ignition system and carburetor, both particular sources of trouble in marine applications. This does not mean that the diesel doesn't need careful attention: It does. Here are the primary areas of attention you should be aware of, even if you have all maintenance procedures done by a mechanic.

Oil Classification

By now it should be patently clear to you that your diesel demands a clean supply of lubricating oil to run long and properly. But equally important is the right type of oil. Lubricating oils are classified by the American Petroleum Institute (API) according to what type of engines they are appropriate for and how advanced their additive package is. Oils are also classified according to the ease with which they flow at a specific temperature. Two typical combined ratings are SE 30W and SF-CD 10W-30.

In terms of API classification, there are two types of engines: spark-ignition engines (gasoline engines) and compression-ignition engines, diesels). An oil rated **S** is designed for use in a gasoline engine while e rated **C** is meant for diesels. Some oils carry dual ratings, such as C, meaning the oil can be used either in gasoline or diesel en-

Do not use an oil rated solely for spark-ignition engines in diesels. It will cause either immediate damage or an increased rate of wear. Make sure that whoever adds or changes your engine's oil uses the appropriate API-classified oil. If the API classification is not clearly visible on the outside of each oil container, select another brand.

The second letter of the API designation represents the complexity of the additive package, typically starting with **A**, the lowest level with the least advanced additives, and progressing alphabetically upward. It is not particularly important to know precisely what additive package is represented by each letter except for two points: First, if your diesel is turbocharged, it requires an oil with the designation CC or higher. Second, as a rule, always use the oil with the highest designation available. In other words, if you have a choice between CC or CD oil, choose CD, regardless of what type of diesel engine you have.

At this time the highest available classification for diesel oils is CD, but lubricating oils are always being researched and improved, and as soon as a better additive package is discovered it will no doubt be implemented and the oil using it will be designated CE. As long as you use the highest rating available, you can't go wrong.

Viscosity Classification

There is one other factor to consider in selecting an oil: its ability to flow freely at a specific temperature, a characteristic commonly referred to as its **weight**, or **viscosity**. Viscosity is designated by an arbitrary number, usually between 5 and 50. The lower the number, the thinner the oil and the easier it will flow when cold. But low-viscosity oil also is less likely to maintain the proper oil film successfully at high temperatures. Higher numbers indicate a thicker, more viscous oil that does not flow as easily when cold but is less likely to become excessively thin when hot.

Some oils carry two viscosity designations, such as 10W-30 (the W stands for weight); these are called **multi-viscosity** oils. A 10W-30 oil has the thickness of a 10-weight oil when it is cold and a 30-weight oil when it is hot. Sound ideal? Some engine builders believe that because more additives must go into the oil to achieve multi-viscosity, some of the oil itself must be displaced, thus reducing lubricative properties. True or not, for most pleasure boats—particularly those powered by diesels—single-viscosity oil is preferable.

The question of single- versus multi-weight oil generally is a moot one anyway because most pleasure boats are not operated either in extremely cold or in extremely hot environments, where "multi-vis" oils have a distinct advantage. Under typical ambient conditions, a single-weight oil, usually a 30W, is sufficient. In any case, check your owner's manual and adhere to its recommendations.

As a general rule, most engine builders do not recommend mixing oils of different viscosities unless it is absolutely necessary. For this reason it's always wise to carry onboard a few one-quart cans of the same oil that's in your engine. Of course if you must add a quart, note it in your log.

When it comes time to change oil, *you* should decide what kind of oil goes into your engine, not your mechanic. Follow the manufacturer's guidelines strictly, and if you have a question, don't hesitate to call the manufacturer or distributor. For instance, if your diesel is using a lot of oil between changes, it may help to go to a heavier weight. But before you do, consult an engine expert to make sure higher-viscosity oil still can do the job.

Speaking of changing oil, many boaters frequently are unsure how often it should be done. Since an oil change in a diesel is a good deal more expensive than in a gasoline engine, most boaters don't want to change too frequently, yet they are aware that an oil change is the single most effective thing they can do to prolong the life of their engine.

Oil Change Interval

To determine the proper service interval, start with your owner's manual. This frequency should be the outside limit only; conditions may warrant less time between oil changes. If your engine has been run unusually hard, has spent a lot of time at idle speeds where it could not always warm up fully, or has been subject to any other unusual operating condition (dust, heavy loads, constant starting and stopping), reduce the interval between oil changes. Note also that, even when oil sits in an engine that has not been run, it must be changed periodically since various acids, moisture, and other contaminants still will accumulate in it. Clearly there's a certain amount of guesswork involved in deciding exactly when to change oil. If you find that bothersome, there is an alternative: oil analysis. (See Chapter 11.)

One final note about oil changes: If you don't know it already you soon will discover that oil filters for diesel engines are significantly more expensive than those for gasoline engines. Not surprisingly then, you will be tempted to change the filter less frequently than the oil—perhaps only every other oil change. *Don't succumb to this temptation!* The oil filter is designed not only to trap dirt but to absorb moisture and other liquid contaminants. At oil change time the filter contains well over a quart of dirty oil that can immediately reduce the benefit of the oil change for which you just paid so dearly. Change the filter every time you change the oil. It's cheap insurance.

Additives and Refiners

As soon as you purchase a diesel engine, someone will try either to sell you an additive to vastly improve the quality of your oil or some device to free you of the drudgery of changing oil altogether. As to the first, engine builders almost universally agree that oil additives are a waste of money. Today's oils contain the best additives available; putting anything more into them either will do little or no good, or might actually cause harm by interfering with this very carefully conceived and executed package.

As for the second, the most common mechanism to avoid oil changes is the so-called oil refiner. Essentially supplementary filters with complex, fine elements and integral heaters to evaporate moisture, oil refiners are widely accepted as effective in extending—but not eliminating—oil change intervals. Unfortunately, such devices are fairly expensive and the average boater may find it difficult to justify the cost of one versus the cost of regular oil changes unless he puts a lot of hours on his engine each year. If someone intent on selling such a unit tries to convince you that these devices actually do a better job of protecting your engine from wear than regular oil and filter changes, you should be skeptical, to say the least.

Caring for Fuel

After oil, the next most important fluid in your engine is fuel. As we've seen, fuel must function not only as a combustible but also as a lubricant and coolant, so diesel fuel must be as pure and clean as possible. This requires that you pay attention to fuel not just before it enters the combustion chamber, but even before it enters the fuel tank.

There are two principal kinds of diesel fuel, Diesel #1 and Diesel #2, the differences being primarily in the degree of refinement and the ease with which they burn at lower temperatures. The designations aren't really important for most boaters operating in North American and European waters; virtually all fuel will be Diesel #2 and thus be sufficient for virtually all noncommercial marine applications. If Diesel #1 is available, it likely will be significantly more expensive and will offer no noticeable improvement in performance or efficiency unless ambient temperatures are well below freezing.

Sulfur and Moisture

Once you leave North America and Europe, however, the situation can change. Third World countries in general, and Latin American and Caribbean countries in particular, are notorious for supplying poor-quality diesel fuel at marinas. In these cases, it is always wise to ask for the highest grade diesel fuel available. In more remote parts of these countries you may find that the only fuel available is kerosene or perhaps even Jet-A. Although these fuels may be acceptable in the short term, they, and indeed all foreign fuels, may contain significantly higher amounts of sulfur than domestic fuels. When too much sulfur is present in diesel fuel it combines with moisture produced during combustion to form sulfuric acid, which can eat away virtually every metal component in the engine.

The average boat owner, particularly one moving from port to port, has no practical method of determining the sulfur content of diesel fuel. Since sulfuric acid accumulates in the lubricating oil, however, oil analysis can tell you when the acid has reached unsafe levels and the oil should be changed. (Most oil analysis labs can provide containers and mailers that can be used outside of the U.S.A.) If oil analysis is impractical, the only solution is to err on the safe side and reduce your oil change interval—perhaps by as much as half—to keep the acids in the oil at a reasonable level.

Another potential problem with diesel fuel that occurs in varying degrees all over the world is the presence of excessive moisture. (In Mexico the problem is so severe that it is not unusual to see station attendants pump fuel from the nozzle directly into the street after receiving a load of fuel to get rid of the accumulated water.) Moisture is inevitable in all fuel, but can be tolerated if amounts remain small. Moisture can accumulate from sloppy handling between the refinery and pump, or simply from condensation produced during the normal atmospheric heating and cooling of tanks.

Water in diesel fuel reduces combustion efficiency, and in sufficient quantities can stop a diesel cold. When this is the case it becomes necessary to bleed the entire fuel system of contaminated fuel, and perhaps drain and clean the fuel tank as well. Clearly this is an expensive, messy, labor-intensive procedure to be scrupulously avoided.

Water also reduces the lubricative properties of the fuel, particularly endangering fuel pumps and injectors. In this instance, the damage may be more gradual and more difficult to spot than with large quantities, but no less worrisome.

Since diesel fuel normally floats on water, most factory-installed filters deal with it by allowing it to accumulate in the bottom of the filter canisters, there to be removed at maintenance time. Some manufacturers have also developed barrier-type filters said to be effective in removing smaller amounts of water. However, agitation can mix water and diesel fuel into an emulsion that is very difficult for barrier-type filters to separate.

The best method of curing an emulsion of water and diesel fuel is to centrifuge it in a fuel/water separator. Such units are available from companies like Racor and Dahl at relatively low cost. They usually feature a transparent bowl in which you can see the actual accumulation of water, as well as a petcock at the bottom of the bowl by which the water can be drained. (If you have such a separator, a visual check of the bowl should be part of your daily checklist.)

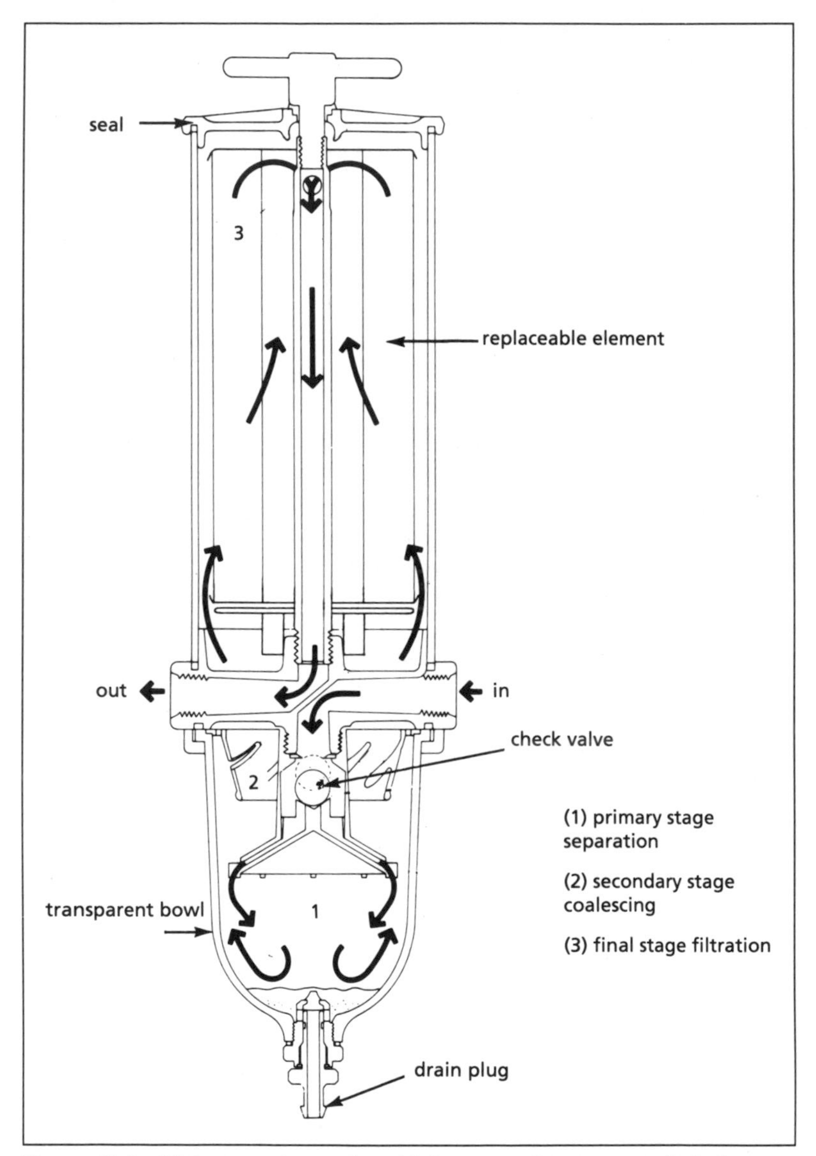

Figure 14-1 Water separators such as this Racor are almost a necessity in the marine environment.

Most fuel/water separators also include an integral barrier filter to remove particulates down to one micron in size, further protecting your fuel system. An additional feature, and one well worth considering, is an automatic alarm that sounds when water in the bowl reaches a pre-set level.

Solid Contaminants

The final problem area with diesel fuel is the presence of particulates, or more simply, dirt. This is the least threatening of the three fuel-related problems because virtually all diesels are equipped at the factory with two fuel filters, the first a relatively coarse barrier (the **primary** filter), the second a finer one (the **secondary** filter). As long as these filters are serviced according to the manufacturer's recommendations, damage from particulates should not be a problem.

You should be aware that if your engine's fuel filters do become clogged, the engine will simply stop, usually with little warning. The

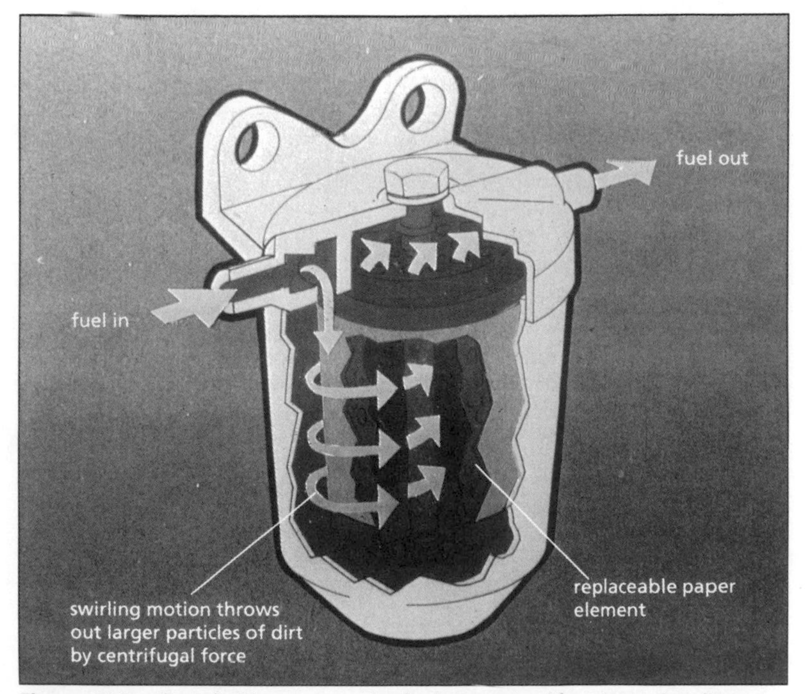

Figure 14-2 Clean fuel is a prerequisite for long engine life. Primary fuel filters such as this are invariably accompanied by a smaller mesh secondary filter.

only way to remedy this disconcerting problem is to change the filter cartridges. You should always have at least a couple of spare cartridges for each filter on board, since if you're unlucky enough to get a load of bad fuel, you easily could go through two filters before you get rid of all the contamination.

Whenever you replace a fuel filter, remember to fill the filter with clean fuel before reassembling it to prevent air from entering the system. (You can usually get fuel by disconnecting a fuel line upstream of the transfer pump, where air will not be introduced into the system.)

If you find your filters are constantly clogging, your problem may not be at the pump; it may be in your fuel tank. Most tanks are designed with the fuel pick-up a few inches off the bottom of the tank. This leaves a dead area in which dirt and heavy contaminants can accumulate without being drawn into the fuel line. If you have an older boat or one with a lot of hours on it (particularly time in foreign waters), your fuel tank may have a layer of contaminants on its bottom that has built up sufficiently to reach the fuel pick up. The only solution is to have the tank either replaced or cleaned. That's a job for a professional.

Additives

One final note about fuel concerns additives. Just as there are dozens of salesmen out there ready to sell you something to "vastly improve" your oil, so are there plenty of hawkers with "miracle" fuel additives that supposedly will double your mileage. As with aftermarket oil additives, these should be approached with a healthy dose of skepticism. In the vast majority of operating environments no fuel additive is necessary, and in some cases one actually may be harmful. There are, however, two notable exceptions:

Diesel fuel is fine as long as it's being used, or at least being moved around. But when it settles, bad things can happen. Believe it or not, there is an algae-like organism that can take root and thrive inside a diesel tank if the fuel is left relatively undisturbed. Once the stuff starts to grow, it is very hard to get rid of.

The only solution usually is a **biocide**, an additive that kills the organism without damaging your fuel system. Great care must be taken in choosing a biocide since some contain alcohol, which does a fine job of killing off the stuff but also reduces the lubricative properties of diesel fuel. If your fuel system needs a biocide—and you'll be able to tell because your fuel filters will be constantly clogged with thick, dark gelatinous stuff—consult your diesel's manufacturer or distributor to determine which product is recommended for your specific engine.

The second instance where a fuel additive is warranted is in boats that are laid up for storage, particularly over the winter. Condensation and biological growth are exacerbated when fuel is left unagitated for extended periods, but winter storage also presents the additional problem of **fuel oxidation**. Simply stated, this occurs when undisturbed fuel is altered chemically after combining with ambient oxygen. The fuel becomes unstable and can form gum, varnish, and other by-products that quickly clog the diesel's delicate fuel system.

The solution to fuel oxidation is the addition of a **fuel stabilizer** whenever you believe your boat will sit undisturbed for more than a month. Fuel stabilizers are formulated to preserve the fuel in its original state. Once again, fuel preservatives come in various types and formulations, not all of which are necessarily good for your diesel engine. The best place to turn for advice concerning a fuel stabilizer for your laid-up boat is again the manufacturer or distributor. Do not rely solely upon advertising claims or buy simply what is being sold at the boatyard, for there is a lot of snake oil on the market today, some of which can end up taking a big bite out of your wallet while failing to live up to its promises.

Caring for the Cooling System

Since the vast majority of marine diesels are freshwater-cooled, caring for the cooling system involves caring for two parts: the raw-water system and the closed-loop cooling system. Caring for the raw-water system starts at the through-hull fitting, on the outside of the boat. Many diesels have overheated for no other reason than the fact that barnacles or other marine growth have accumulated around the through-hull fitting, restricting the opening and resulting in insufficient water flow to the pump and heat exchangers. If your hull bottom has been coated with the correct antifouling paint and if you were careful to apply the paint at least a few inches inside the through-hull fittings, an annual inspection at haul-out should be sufficient. Make sure that, when growth is scraped or pressure-washed off the hull at haul-out, a screwdriver or similar narrow scraper is also used to remove any growth inside the through-hull fitting.

Most modern diesel-powered pleasure boats are equipped with sea-water strainers. These glass- or plastic-enclosed filters, usually attached to the inside of the through-hull fitting, are designed to prevent any ingested material from reaching the heat exchangers, where it might clog their small openings. In many large installations, such strainers have been eliminated because the raw-water pump is of such size that it can grind up any material small enough to enter the through-hull fitting.

If your boat is equipped with a sea-water strainer, you should check it periodically for material that might accumulate and either clog it or restrict the flow of water through it. Often this can be done by a simple visual check, but at least two or three times each year you should ac-

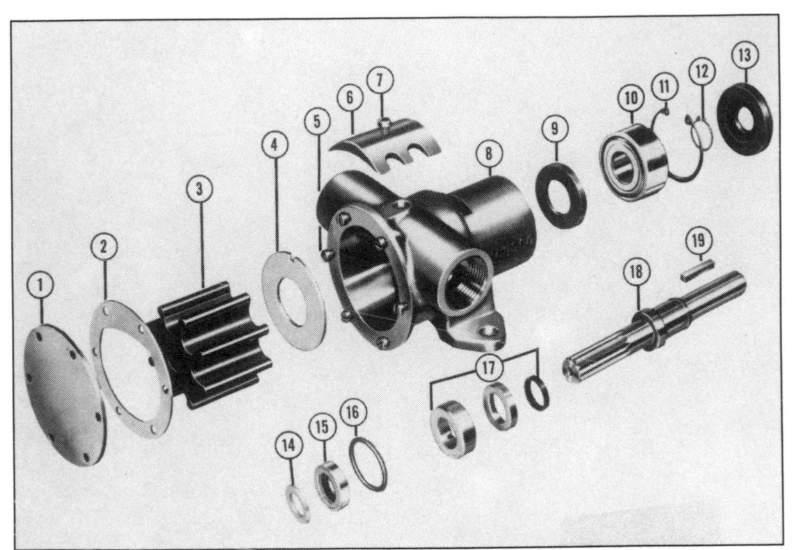

Figure 15-1 An exploded view of a rubber-impeller–type raw-water pump.

tually unscrew the strainer's two wingnuts, remove the top, and pull out the internal metal basket to make sure there is nothing in it.

The Raw-Water Pump

The next point of care in a diesel's cooling system is the raw-water pump. Most pumps consist of a rubber or synthetic impeller inside a case of brass or some other relatively inert metal. The most likely point of failure is the impeller, but incipient failure is often difficult, if not impossible, to detect visually.

Most maintenance experts agree that the potential problems created by disassembling a raw-water pump and removing the impeller and inspecting it are greater than any potential benefit. Unless you have reason to believe that the impeller may have had to endure a fair amount of solid material or that for some reason it has run dry for any length of time, it is better simply to leave it alone. If you insist on checking it, make it a once-a-year procedure.

The best way to determine when the raw-water pump is not operating correctly is to form a mental image of the normal amount of water discharged from the boat, either through the exhaust system or out a separate through hull. Most commercial captains can tell at a glance when the outflow of water from their boat's exhaust is below par, and you should be able to do the same. This can warn you well ahead of an engine alarm that something is amiss.

Figure 15-2 Sacrificial zinc pencils should be checked frequently and replaced as needed. You'll find them in the heat exchangers and exhaust risers. Check your owner's manual and make sure you locate them all. Pull each zinc and tap it lightly with a hammer; if it flakes apart, replace it.

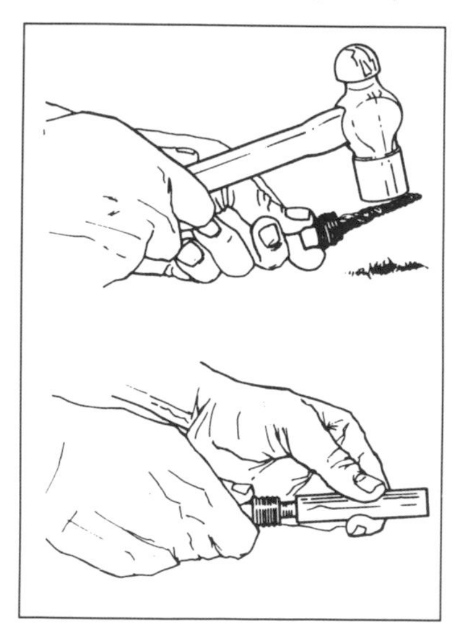

The Heat Exchangers

The last place you need to check in the raw-water system is the heat exchanger. As we've noted previously, each heat exchanger in the system should have at least one sacrificial zinc pencil designed to corrode away before the exchanger does. It's important not only to check these periodically, but to replace them whenever they become more than half eroded. Keep a supply of zincs aboard and make sure you know the location of each one within your engine's cooling circuit. When in doubt, replace a zinc with a new one.

There are two things that require close supervision in a diesel's coolant circuit. One is, of course, the coolant. It should be monitored both for proper level and for proper concentration. As we've said earlier, the addition of a coolant recovery bottle can make checking the coolant level a breeze, and there are inexpensive testers available that show at a glance the concentration of antifreeze in the cooling system.

You should check whether your engine distributor or manufacturer recommends a supplementary water conditioner or anti-rust additive. Some engines may even be equipped with a separate filter for the cooling system. Whatever the case with your engine, follow the engine builder's recommendations faithfully. And remember that all coolants and additives degrade with use and time: Check them periodically for effectiveness.

You should find recommendations for draining and changing your diesel's coolant in your owner's manual. As with oil change recommendations, consider these to be the *maximum* allowable intervals. Any sign of rust, corrosion, or contamination demands draining, flushing with the appropriate chemical, and refilling with fresh coolant in the specified proportion.

The other point on your engine's freshwater system worthy of special notice is the **thermostat**. Designed to maintain as even an operating temperature as possible in your engine, the thermostat is subjected to thousands of openings and closings over its life. Although a relatively simple mechanism, it eventually will fail and when it does the failure may or may not be obvious. A thermostat that fails to open at the correct temperature or one that fails to open fully will eventually result in an overheated engine. One that fails to close fully or to close sufficiently relative to coolant temperature can result in an engine that fails to reach proper operating temperature. In either case, a failed thermostat can render your engine inoperative, so it's always wise to carry a spare.

Installation techniques vary from engine to engine, but basically involve removal of a couple of bolts and the water neck, removal of the old thermostat (making careful note of how it was installed), careful cleaning and removal of the old gasket, and reinstallation of a new gasket and thermostat. Gasket sealant is usually not required on modern engines, but check your engine manual for specific recommendations.

One final cautionary note: Check occasionally for the presence of oil in your engine's coolant. Although rare, it can occur and signals a failed head gasket or cracked block. Oil in the coolant is a sign of severe trouble and demands immediate, professional attention.

Doing It Yourself

For a variety of reasons, including saving money and the simple joy of doing it yourself, a lot of boaters would prefer to do the maintenance chores on their diesels. Unfortunately, many shy away from the task not because of laziness but because of concern that the job may be too difficult. In truth, the procedures involved in maintaining a diesel aren't really much different from those used in maintaining your automobile. The primary difference is one of scale.

Simply stated, a diesel has more of everything and most everything it has costs more. That doesn't mean you can't do the work; you'll just have to be better prepared.

Oil

We've already discussed how to choose the right oil; now let's talk about how to change it. First, never change oil when it's cold: It won't flow freely and it will be difficult to get all the dirty oil out of the engine. The engine doesn't have to be hot—warm is fine.

When you want to change the oil in your automobile you simply slide a container under the oil pan, remove the drain plug, and let the oil run out. Unfortunately, that procedure is unlikely to work in most diesel-powered boats for a variety of reasons:

- First, you probably can't get to the drain plug.
- Second, there probably isn't a flat spot under the engine on which you could set a container.
- Third, you're going to be draining perhaps two to three times as much oil as you would from your car, so you'd need a pretty big container.

One solution is to pump the warm oil out of the oil pan through the dipstick hole. The mechanism commonly used for this is a simple centrifugal pump that fits on the end of an electric drill. You snake the inlet tube down the oil pan and place the outlet tube into a large container, such as a five-gallon pail. Flip on the drill and wait for the flow of oil to stop.

You'll probably be waiting quite a while, as the pumping capacity of these units is pretty slim. Another drawback to this technique is that the tube you snaked down the dipstick hole may or may not actually reach the lowest point of the oil pan; in other words, you may or may not get out all the oil.

A better solution is to install an oil pump kit directly on your engine. If the drain plug is accessible, it is removed and a hard copper line attached in its place, at the lowest point. The line is connected to a battery-operated, high-capacity pump that can do the job in just a few minutes. Just place the outlet hose in a container, switch on the pump, and sit back and wait. The system is more expensive that the battery-operated drill pump, but it's worth it, especially since you'll get virtually all the oil that's in the pan.

If the drain plug is inaccessible, some hybrid systems are available with a relatively firm tube, which should get pretty close to the bottom of the pan, and a higher-capacity pump that can be attached to your boat's battery with alligator clips. Check with the local chandlery.

Once you have a full container of dirty oil you have to decide what to do with it. This can be a real problem in some places, although many states now require that anyone who sells oil must accept used oil in return. This shouldn't even require mentioning, but unfortunately it does: *Don't pour the oil on the ground, down the sewer, or into the water.* If you need a reason why, you shouldn't own a boat.

Many boat owners pour the used oil back into the original containers and store them in a safe place until their municipality has an annual "Amnesty Day," in which toxic chemicals are accepted for disposal. Some service stations accept used oil, and there are oil-recovery firms in many urban areas; check your Yellow Pages under "Oils—Waste." With a little perseverance, you can find a proper place to get rid of your oil.

Oil Filters

Chances are your car has a spin-on oil filter designed to be discarded completely when removed. On the other hand, your diesel probably has a replaceable cartridge within a metal canister, although some smaller diesels may be equipped with automotive-style spin-on filters. Regardless, your first concern should be procuring the proper oil filter. For your car, you can simply run down to K-Mart and pick up whatever's on sale. If you could find someone that sold discount diesel parts (unlikely), you could do the same, but it's really not a good idea. The diesel oil filter is called upon to do a lot more than its automotive counterpart, so your best move is to buy filters from a recognizable company such as Fram or AC. Don't scrimp. (You may be able to save money buying oil filters—and oil—in bulk, perhaps from a local truck stop, since truck filters usually are identical to marine filters.)

Check your owner's manual to see if you should fill the filter or canister with clean oil before you install it. Many mechanics do this anyway if the position of the oil filter allows it, as it keeps the engine from running dry for the first few seconds after an oil change. If you choose to do the same, remember to keep track of how much oil you add. Overfilling a diesel with oil can be both messy and dangerous.

As you would with your car, you must ensure that the filter is sealed properly when installed. If the filter is a spin-on unit, this usually means the same procedure as your car: Apply a thin film of clean oil on the rubber gasket, then tighten the filter firmly by hand. If the filter is a cartridge unit, the cartridge may or may not have a gasket, which usually will seat itself. Most assuredly there will be an O-ring gasket on the exterior canister that must be properly seated. Many mechanics replace this seal every time they change the element to minimize the chance of leakage. Since O-rings are relatively inexpensive, this practice is probably good insurance. If you're unsure how to install the gasket (it's really quite obvious), ask the person who sells it to you to demonstrate.

After you change the filter be sure the exterior of the unit is absolutely clean so you'll be able to detect any leakage quickly. If you do your own maintenance on your car, you may be used to a somewhat dirty engine, a fact of life because it's exposed to road grime. Dirt should never be tolerated on a marine engine. The engine, all its components, and the surrounding environment (including the bilge) should be scrupulously clean, not only to help you determine when something is wrong but for safety reasons as well. Remember, your car's engine is exposed to the open air; your boat's engine operates in a relatively closed environment where sloppiness can lead to pollution, slips, and even fire.

Once you have the oil filter in place, start the engine and let it run long enough for the oil to warm. Check for leaks. If there are none, this part of your job is finished—except, of course, for finding a proper way to dispose of the dirty oil filter.

Fuel Filters

One thing you probably don't have to do on your car (or at least not very often) that you do on a diesel is change the fuel filters. As we've said, there usually are two, and both should be changed each time the

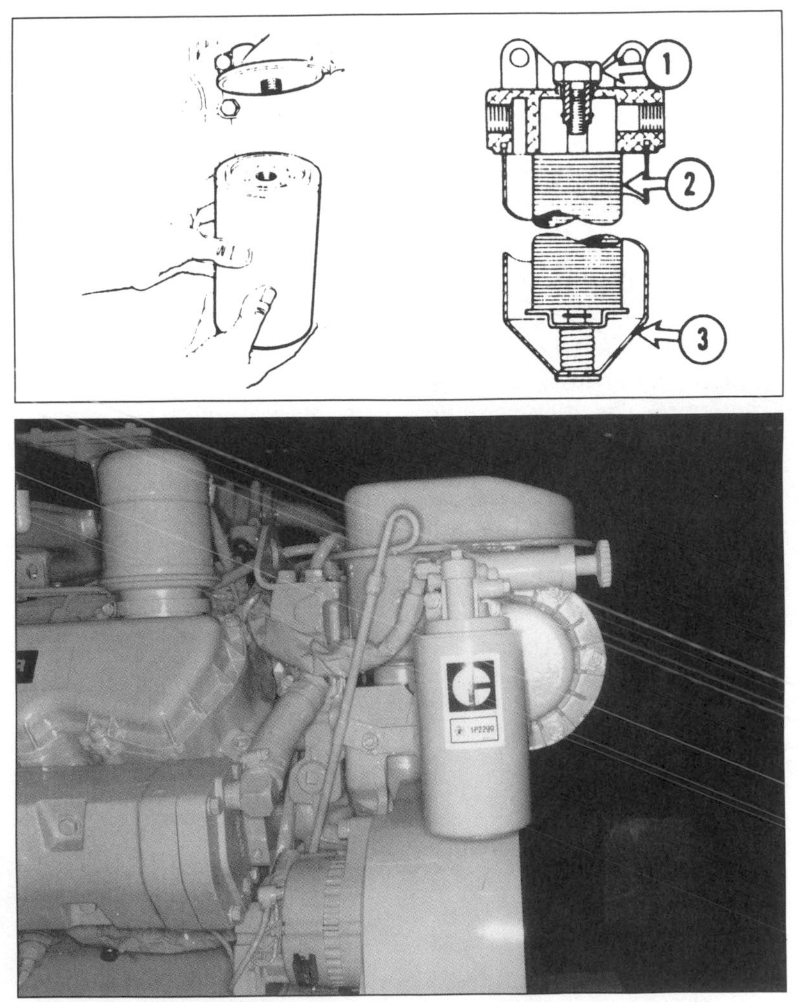

Figure 16-1 Many primary fuel filters—and most oil filters—are replaceable cartridges contained within a metal cannister. (1) retaining screw; (2) filter element; (3) metal canister. Spin-on filters (bottom) are used for most secondary fuel filters and a few primaries. Be sure to wipe the rubber gasket clean, fill with clean fuel or oil, and leave a thin film of fuel or oil when reinstalling both types of filters.

oil is changed. (Many boaters who have installed a fuel/water separator upstream of these two filters forgo changing them every time and instead just change the filter in the separator, the theory being that the fuel reaching the two original equipment filters is already clean.) On most engines, one filter will be coarse and the other fine, so it is im perative that they not be mixed up. The coarser filter is always the farther upstream of the two.

Use the same care in purchasing and installing a fuel filter that you did with the oil filter. Since diesel fuel is more flammable than oil, you should be even more watchful for leaks. Also, while priming the oil filter may be optional, it is mandatory on the fuel filter. You should *always* fill the filter full of fuel before installing it. Air simply cannot be allowed to enter the diesel fuel system.

Other Service

After oil and filters, the only other periodic service required for your diesel engine might be cleaning the crankcase ventilator, if so equipped, and topping off fluids, including in the hydraulic pump, if so equipped. The primary cautions here are to use only the approved fluids and solvents, which should be listed in your owner's manual.

Some older diesels may also have grease fittings or other lubrication points, such as at the throttle linkage. Again, check your owner's manual for specifications.

If you live in cold climates, you will probably have to change to either a lighter weight or multi-viscosity oil at some point each year, and if it's *really* cold, you may even have to switch to Diesel #1. Check your owner's manual.

Many boat owners living in cold climates also must prepare their diesel for winter lay-up. This is another procedure you either can do yourself or leave to a mechanic. Basically, diesel engine winterization entails removing any water (not coolant) from the engine cooling system, ensuring that the coolant is of sufficient concentration to protect against freezing, changing the oil and filter, topping off the fuel tanks to prevent condensation, and adding a fuel stabilizer. For more specific recommendations, check your engine owner's manual.

At this point, you will have done about all the scheduled maintenance you can perform on a marine diesel without requiring a shop manual or specialized tools. Your engine may, for example, require periodic adjustment to valves and tappets. This will require feeler gauges and a manual to tell you how to rotate the crankshaft and when to adjust each cylinder.

Some engines may require adjustment of the fuel system, either a centralized pump or unit injectors. Both of these devices demand extremely high tolerances; no one but a highly trained technician should do this work. Indeed, even the most skilled mechanics usually will remove the pump or unit injectors and send them to a separate facility where they can be tested and adjusted on a special calibration stand. *o not tamper with your diesel's fuel system, even if you have a anual.*

If you already own a diesel, you've probably heard of the diesel tune-up, an annual procedure touted by many mechanics as essential to the health and well-being of your diesel. Ask what is involved in a diesel tune-up and usually you'll be told that in addition to oil and filter changes, necessary adjustments are conducted on the fuel system.

The truth is that there is no such thing as a diesel tune-up. Check your owner's manual and you'll see precisely what maintenance procedures are required. Unless there is something wrong with your diesel engine, no additional work should be required. Indeed, a good diesel mechanic will tell you that as a rule—and especially with regard to the diesel fuel system—the less tampering the better.

How to Choose and Deal with a Mechanic

Selecting a diesel mechanic is like selecting a physician: you don't really want one but you know you need one, and you're unsure about how to choose one because you don't know much about the discipline. This is why doctors—and mechanics—named Adams fare better than those named Zimmerman: The natural tendency is to rely on alphabetical order when all else is lost.

There are ways to tell good mechanics from bad, but shopping for the best deal is not one of them. There are plenty of good mechanics that charge a low hourly rate and just as many bad ones that charge a high hourly rate. If you find a mechanic that works cheap, he may be so incompetent that it takes him twice as long to do the job. We'll deal more with the financial aspects of diesel mechanics in a moment. Right now, let's talk about how to find a good mechanic.

The first rule of dealing with a mechanic is *don't be intimidated.* It's true, you know a lot less about diesels than he, but never forget that you're the one paying the bills—*you* should be in the driver's seat. Never be afraid to ask a mechanic anything or to challenge him when you're dissatisfied with his answer. If you learn just one thing—deal with a mechanic from a position of strength and authority—you will have gone a long way toward getting your money's worth

Once you start looking for a mechanic your first source should be word of mouth. If you have a friend with a diesel-powered boat, ask him if he's happy with his mechanic. Also ask the yard foreman, the man who sold you the boat, and those whose boats are moored around you. If you get a rousing recommendation from any of them, check the guy out. If you get two or three opinions that agree, you're in real luck. The next step should be to meet with the mechanic before you actually call him for work. Ideally, the meeting will take place at his shop so you can have a look around. Being a diesel mechanic is a dirty job, but that doesn't preclude neatness. If he's a slob and his tool box looks like a kid's toy chest, he's disorganized at best and a poor mechanic at worst. And if he doesn't have time to talk to you, forget him.

When you speak to a mechanic, ask him about his training and experience. Any factory training is certainly a plus, although no guarantee of success. Recurrent training in specialized areas is a sign that he takes his profession seriously and wants to stay abreast of new developments.

Discuss your specific engine and boat with him and note how he listens. A lot of mechanics have little or no respect for an owner, and you can tell that in the way they listen. Stay away from them, no matter how expert they may seem, or they'll end up directing your life. If the mechanic expresses some familiarity with your engine or boat, that's a good sign. More important, however, is his overall attitude. Does he seem reasonable, interested, and fair-minded, as well as being competent?

In the end, you really need to know more about human nature than diesel engines to choose a mechanic. Don't be afraid to rely on your impressions and instincts. The truth is, good mechanics are hard to find, and finding them often is as much a matter of serendipity as forethought.

What's a Fair Fee?

Mechanics generally compute their charges one of two ways: One is the standard rate method where, by referring to a book, a mechanic can tell how much time it should take (theoretically) to perform a certain task. He simply multiplies that time by his hourly rate and gets the estimated charges. If he gets the job done faster you still pay the estimated rate; if it takes longer he'll charge you more. The standard rate method is most common in large shops.

The other method is simply to multiply how long it takes to complete the job by the hourly rate. This sounds simple, but there are variations on the theme. For instance, some mechanics show up at a job cold, with no parts and perhaps not even the correct tools. They then proceed to charge you for the time it takes them to travel to and from the shop or parts house, and if that weren't enough, they may even plug in a markup on the parts. Naturally, a mechanic legitimately could find he needs an unanticipated part or tool after getting into a job, but generally this bare-bones approach is a rip-off.

You should be able to get firm estimates for most scheduled maintenance and for most common types of repairs. But understand that a boat is not like a car: Every installation varies slightly. If it takes a mechanic longer to pull an injector out of your engine because the boatbuilder mounted some overhead duct work on top of the valve cover, you'll have to pay for it. If, however, a mechanic refuses to give you any firm estimates for scheduled maintenance, you probably should look for another mechanic.

Although it's probably too late to save you (from making a bad choice) at this point, a look at a mechanic's invoice can tell you a lot about the quality of his work. Check the amount of hours posted. It's normal to round off time, but if he's rounding off 2 1/2 hours to 3 hours, you're getting ripped off.

Note the prices for parts. This is where many mechanics really pad their bills. If a price seems too high, don't hesitate to ask about it. If the explanation seems inadequate, call a local parts house and verify the cost. You have to expect *some* markup, but anything over 25 percent is cause for questioning.

Another potential trouble spot is in the miscellaneous category, sometimes referred to as "shop materials." Originally this was intended to cover incidentals, such as shop towels, grease, and miscellaneous chemicals, but often it develops into just another way to jack up the bill. You shouldn't hesitate to ask about this charge either, particularly if it exceeds $25.

Don't be reticent about asking to see any old parts that were replaced. This is not being rude, it's just being a smart customer. If a raw-water impeller looks perfectly fine to you, ask the mechanic to explain why he replaced it. If his explanation seems implausible, don't pay for it.

And finally, don't pay for any unauthorized work. It isn't unusual for a mechanic to say, "I know we didn't talk about it but once I got inside I thought this should be replaced." Tell him ahead of time to speak to you before he does any work you haven't already specified. Just making that statement will make him think twice about padding the work.

Most mechanics are honest, hardworking individuals, but as in every other profession there are exceptions. Armed with a working knowledge of the diesel engine and a healthy dose of cynicism, chances are you'll never have to worry about being someone's patsy.

Basic Tools and Spare Parts

This book is specifically designed for the layman, the boat owner who prefers to leave major engine work to an expert. But even the most uninvolved owner will need to carry a few well-chosen parts and tools aboard, if only to get out of a jam. The tools should fit easily into a small toolbox and the parts should take up no more than a corner of your engine compartment.

Tools

There are two ways to proceed in setting up a tool kit. You can simply go to one of the tool outlets like Sears, get one of the 100-piece mechanic's tool kits, and keep it aboard. That will certainly cover most of your needs. Or, if you're more cost- and space-conscious, you can pick only those you think you are most likely to need. In either case, purchase good-quality tools, not the kind you pull out of a bargain bin for 99 cents each. (Note that the recommendations that follow apply to your diesel engine only; other tools may be necessary for the rest of your boat.)

Your basic tool kit should begin with a complete socket wrench set, from 1/4 to 3/4 inch, along with such accessories as a ratchet, a couple of drive extensions, a universal joint, and a breaker bar (a long handle designed to be placed over the ratchet handle to provide extra leverage). You'll note that socket sets come in a variety of drive sizes and in either deep or standard socket design. You'll probably get the most use from standard-depth sockets, and find the 1/2-inch drive is easiest to work with.

In addition to socket wrenches, bring along a couple of adjustable wrenches, one 6-inch and one 12-inch. Many mechanics sneer at such wrenches but they've gotten a lot of novices out of many a jam. There's nothing wrong with an adjustable wrench as long as you buy a top-quality one. For smaller work, you might consider a nut driver, a sort of screwdriver/mini-socket wrench combo, with sockets down to at least 1/4 inch. A mid-sized pipe wrench is good for exerting extra leverage and for dealing with rounded-off nuts.

Three pairs of pliers are a good idea: a standard pair, a pair of needle-nosed pliers, and—what is perhaps the most versatile tool in your kit—a pair of Vise-Grips. A pair of offset long-handle pliers (sometimes called water-pump pliers) is optional.

Include a set of both standard and Phillips-head screwdrivers, and an extra-small version of each. A medium-sized paint scraper is handy for removing gaskets, and an old paintbrush can help remove debris from whatever you're working on. Check your owner's manual to see if you also need a special wrench to remove your oil and fuel filters, and you'll always find a use for a small-beam, high-intensity flashlight. One especially handy item around boats is an extendable magnetic pick-up, for all those nuts and bolts you'll inevitably drop into the bilge. Finally, bring along a tape measure, a sharp knife, and a hammer, preferably a medium-sized ball-peen machinist's hammer.

This constitutes a basic tool kit, the kind needed to perform most of the basic maintenance procedures. If you're planning on more extensive work, or if you just want to be prepared for any eventuality, you may also want to include a set of combination wrenches (box- and open-end), one or two cold chisels, a prick punch, and a set of feeler gauges. A quick check with your local engine distributor will also get you a list of specialized tools (and a shop manual) for your type and make of engine.

If you do your boating in salt water, take steps to ensure your tools don't corrode from the salt air. Look for a toolbox with a tight-fitting lid, or better, a gasketed cover. Wipe all tools down occasionally with an oil-soaked rag to help repel moisture.

In addition to tools, you'll want a few other items in your tool kit. Most important are a can of lightweight, all-purpose oil, like WD-40, and rolls of both electrical and duct tape. A small piece of medium-grit sandpaper is handy for cleaning up metal surfaces. Also include a small tube of silicone sealant. Although effective in stopping leakage, it also functions well as an all-purpose adhesive. Best of all, it's easily removable. Other items worth bringing along are an assortment of hose clamps (stainless steel only, including the bolt), and an assortment of bolts, nuts, washers, and self-tapping screws. An inexpensive circuit tester can be a big help in tracking down electrical maladies. And please don't forget that shop manual; even if you never intend to sit down and read it, you may find that some day you'll need it.

Parts

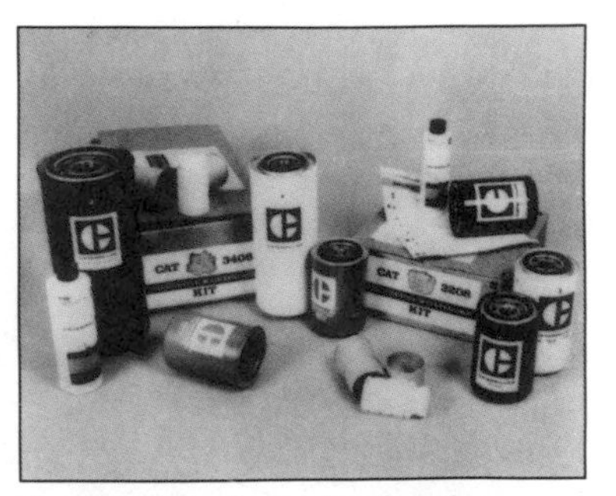

Figure 18-1 Some diesel engine manufacturers sell packaged parts kits that are easy to keep aboard; they might be a lifesaver if you break down in a remote area. Cat's PM kit (left) includes everything you need for scheduled maintenance: all filters, cooling system conditioner, and oil sample bottle and mailer. Tune-up kits (right) include injector nozzles and instructions.

You have to make a basic philosophical decision up front regarding spare parts: Do you want to carry every conceivable part that could break during the course of a trip? Or can you be content to bring along only the essentials? If you're not likely to be more than a half-day's run from port (and parts), I suggest you conserve space and carry just the basics. These include plenty of fuel filter cartridges, an oil filter cartridge, sufficient oil for about a change and a half, and replacement cartridges for your fuel/water separator, if so equipped. Include with all these whatever gaskets and O-rings are appropriate. Also important are at least one, and preferably two, raw-water pump impellers (including gaskets), a thermostat (for the freshwater coolant system), and an assortment of zincs.

Many boaters also bring along one spare injector and whatever gaskets and installation tools go along with it, but this is only practical if you know how to remove and install an injector nozzle. If you don't, you could end up in worse shape than when you started. The procedure is a complex one and you should review it carefully before you even consider attempting this job. (If you decide to do the work, you may also need to bring along a torque wrench.) If you include an injector nozzle, make sure it is covered with a light film of oil and enclosed in a sealed container to prevent corrosion.

Whatever parts you bring should be rotated into use to prevent them from degrading in storage. For instance, if you keep a couple of oil filters on board, the next time you change oil, use one out of your stock and replace it with a new filter. That way all of your parts will be fresh and ready for use every time you need them.

Basic Troubleshooting

I can't give you specific instructions on how to fix your marine diesel engine. Any attempt at that would be futile if for no other reason than each diesel model is slightly different from the others. Any comprehensive troubleshooting instructions would be either prohibitively long or so vague as to be useless.

Instead, I'll concentrate on a brief philosophical discussion about the art of troubleshooting, and I'll give you a few basic questions to ask before you call a mechanic. If you're looking for something more specific, purchase the shop manual for your particular diesel model. Most manuals include a comprehensive troubleshooting chart that can walk you through virtually any problem.

Despite the vast array of sophisticated testing equipment available, your senses remain your most valuable diagnostic tools; odd sounds or odors, hot surfaces, or the color of the engine's exhaust can announce problems long before they appear on gauges.

Get to know the sound of your engine. When you hear something out of the ordinary, pay attention. A loud knocking, for instance, could signal a bad connecting rod—or just an engine hatch left ajar. A strong odor could indicate a fuel leak, an overheating engine, or an electrical problem. You often can locate the source of an overheating problem by feeling—with extreme caution—for hot and cold spots.

Your eyes can be helpful as well. One of the best ways to tell how a diesel is running is by the color of its exhaust, an accurate diagnostic technique when used with certain limitations in mind. Remember that because a marine diesel mixes water with its exhaust, the exhaust is more difficult to read than a standard diesel. Remember also that black smoke is normal under heavy acceleration or other intermittent heavy loads. The duration of the color is important.

Those parameters in mind, two colors of exhaust indicate problems: black and blue. Black exhaust indicates either too much fuel or not enough air. Two possible explanations for black exhaust could be either a clogged air intake or an improperly adjusted fuel system. Blue smoke indicates that oil is burning in the combustion chamber. Possible causes here could be worn piston rings or cylinder walls, worn valve guides, or a clogged crankcase ventilator. If your engine is emitting blue smoke, the first step should be to check the engine log for indications of unusual oil consumption. If that is indicated, the next step is a compression check of each cylinder.

Troubleshooting is really nothing more than a logical process of elimination, but to do it well you must have at least a basic knowledge of how a diesel works. If you've read this book, you know enough about a diesel to troubleshoot it. Here are five simple questions to ask that probably will unearth almost any problem:

Have All the Simplest Things Been Done?

If you remember only one lesson from this chapter, this is the one to remember: The diesel engine is an incredibly reliable and durable piece of machinery; throughout your tenure as its master it's unlikely that it will ever actually break. More often, the problem will be that you have overlooked some minor detail that has caused the engine to malfunction. There is an unalterable human desire to find a macro reason for a macro problem, when more often it's just a simple glitch that's put you out of service. Think small.

For instance, suppose your diesel simply stops running. Before you suspect that the crankshaft has broken in two, walk yourself back through the most basic steps in starting a diesel. Is the key on? (Yes, you turned it on, but has it been turned off inadvertently?) Is there fuel in the tank? (The gauge says there is, but are you sure the fuel gauge is accurate or even working?) Is the fuel getting from the tank to the engine? (Did you remember to turn the fuel valve back on after you changed the filter?)

The key here is always to look at the most basic (and therefore the least likely) cause for a problem. Resist the urge to pick up a tool or call a mechanic. Don't panic. Think logically and sequentially. In the majority of cases, you'll find the culprit is not-so-obvious but so simple as to be truly embarrassing.

Has Anything Changed?

If your diesel ran fine yesterday but shows no signs of life today, ask yourself if anything has been done in the interim. Have you put fuel in it? If so, maybe the fuel is contaminated. Have you or a mechanic worked on it? If the answer is yes, resist the next most common step: "But that couldn't have anything to do with it."

For instance, suppose your diesel refuses to start, but it started fine yesterday. The only thing that happened over the last 24 hours is that you changed the oil. But how could an oil change cause a diesel to quit? Retrace your steps in the engine room and you may find that you inadvertently nudged a fuel valve closed or knocked a wire loose.

Here's an all-too-common example: You just changed your fuel filters and suddenly the engine quits; yet the tank is full of fuel. What's the problem? The odds-on favorite here is air in the fuel system, and you'll need to bleed it. Either pull out the manual or call a mechanic.

The point is that diesel engines rarely just quit when left unattended.

Does It Have Fuel?

Suppose you've asked yourself the first two questions and the answers have not revealed a solution. Now it's time to look deeper for a solution. The first step is to make sure your diesel has what it needs. If you've read this book you know that means clean fuel and air and a supply of electricity. Once again, as you ask these questions, start with the simplest explanations first and use your God-given logical mind.

A fuel/water separator is not only valuable as a means of keeping your fuel clean, it's a great diagnostic tool, too. Look at the clear bowl. If it's empty, you've got a fuel supply problem somewhere between it and the tank. If it's full of fuel but the fuel is cloudy or dark, chances are your problem is a clogged fuel filter. Get out the spare cartridges and wrench-es and start replacing. If the bowl is full of clean fuel, it's reasonable to expect the problem is farther downstream.

If you don't have a fuel/water separator, your job will be more difficult. Using simple logic, you know that fuel comes from the tank, enters one fuel filter, then another, then exits and is pumped on to the injector pump or unit injectors. If you remove the fine filter (the second one) and it's empty, you know either that the first filter is clogged or there's a problem somewhere farther upstream (like no fuel in the tank). Removing the coarse filter may help you decide. Conversely, if the second filter is full of clean fuel, your problem either is downstream in the fuel system (which probably means you need a mechanic) or the problem's not with the fuel system at all.

Does It Have Air?

It seems almost inconceivable that a diesel could fail to run because it lacks air, but it happens. Many a new diesel has quit because the air cleaner became clogged with dirt and debris left over from construction.

As with the fuel system, tracking down an air-related problem is a process of elimination. Make sure you start outside the engine room. Are the engine room vents clear or has some creature chosen them for a nesting spot, restricting the air flow? That solved, the next logical step is the air cleaner. Simply removing it and holding it up to strong light should tell you if it's clean enough to allow air to pass.

If your engine is turbocharged, you'll next want to remove the air cleaner to inspect the exhaust turbine. Don't spin it; just nudge it with your finger to see if it moves freely. If your diesel's had a few hot shutdowns, the turbocharger bearing may be burned and the shaft frozen, rendering the compressor motionless and preventing a sufficient supply of air from reaching the cylinders.

If you own a Detroit Diesel, there is one more place to search before you call a mechanic. It's so simple and so frequently the cause of engine "failure" that it actually should go to the top of your checklist. It's the emergency shutdown, a flapper valve located in the intake manifold that, when shut, closes off the cylinders from any incoming air. It's activated by a T-shaped handle, usually located at the helm, and the tricky part is that once the handle is pulled, the flapper stays closed even if the handle is shoved back in. To reset the flapper you must go down to the engine and manually flip it back into place. A visual check of the helm by itself may deceive you.

Does It Have Electricity?

As we've said before, one of the great things about the diesel is that it doesn't need an electrical ignition system to operate. But that doesn't mean it can do without electricity altogether.

Most obvious is the need for voltage to turn the starter motor. If you turn the key and nothing happens, check your battery voltage gauge. If it's OK, check your vapor-proof battery selector switches. If they're in the right position, it's time to climb below and look for loose connections between battery and starter motor. If everything is tight, look for blown fuses or popped circuit breakers. If they're OK, chances are you need a new starter motor.

There is one other kind of electrical malady that throws a lot of boat owners for a loop. Because a diesel has no electrical ignition system the only way to shut it off is by cutting the supply of fuel. This no mally is done through an electrical solenoid valve that, when en gized by the ignition key, opens and allows fuel to enter the inj pump or unit injectors. If this valve is faulty or the connection bad, the engine will crank and appear to have plenty of clean f air, but it simply won't fire. Determining the problem is at the fuel solenoid is, at least for the layman, usually a process of elimination.

Overheating

One final problem you may someday have to troubleshoot is overheating. Again, the key is to proceed sequentially. First, is water coming into the boat past the through-hull? (Check the raw-water strainer.) Second, is the raw-water pump functioning? (Is the outlet side cold? Is water coming out of the exhaust?) Are the heat exchangers clogged? (Are they too hot to touch?) Is there sufficient coolant in the engine? (*DON'T REMOVE THE CAP!* Check the coolant recovery bottle or wait until the engine cools.)

There are literally thousands more questions you could ask in your quest to find the gremlin in your engine, and whatever your predicament, the key is to proceed slowly and logically. Never skip a step. If you can't find the problem by an orderly, sequential process of elimination, the chances are good that you have a fairly serious problem. That means it's time to quit playing detective and call in an expert.

Index